The ABC's of Memoir
A Primer for Writing Your Life Story

By Sharon K. Ferrett

The Press at Cal Poly Humboldt

Dedicated to the memory of my parents and grandparents. Thank you for your resilience, courage and sheer grit. You made my comfortable life possible and gave me a wonderful childhood.

The Press at Cal Poly Humboldt
Editing by Kyle Morgan
Typesetting by Wilder Yaconelli
Design by Juno Leone and Sarah Godlin
1 Harpst Street
Arcata, CA 95521
ISBN: 978-1-962081-36-8

TABLE OF CONTENTS

Introduction: Why I Wrote This Book..vii

ABC's..1

Appendix..53

About the Author...103

"Life can only be understood backwards; but it must be lived forwards."
-Keirkegaard

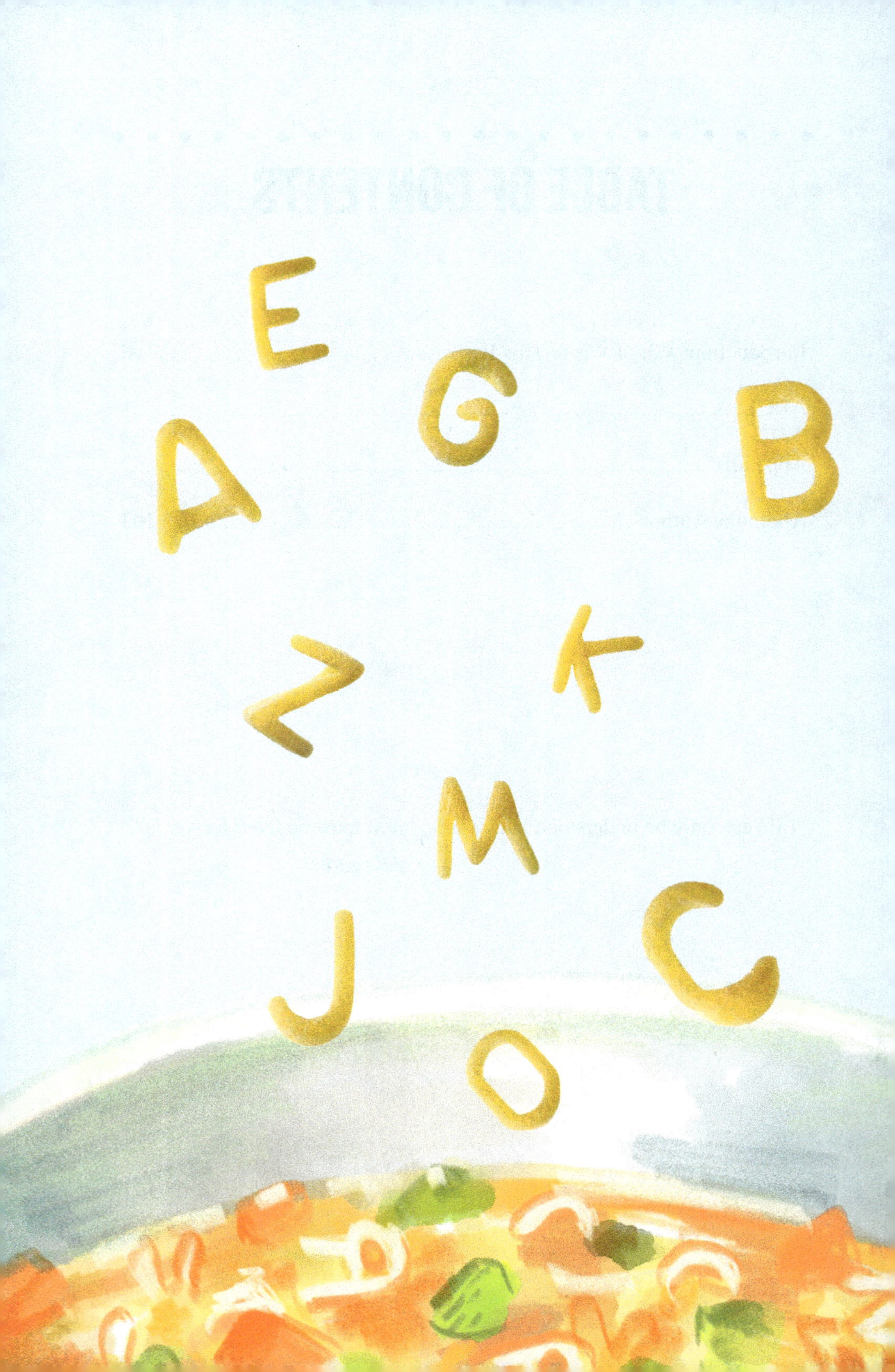

Sharon K. Ferrett

INTRODUCTION

WHY I WROTE THIS BOOK

The idea for this book came many years ago when I received a letter from a man who was serving time in prison and had read my book, Peak Performance. He wrote about the poor choices he had made and his desire to share the lessons he had learned with others. He wanted to tell his story, make sense of his life and to help others avoid bad choices. He wrote, "I was a good kid until I got into drugs and that was the turning point where my life spiraled downward. I have lessons to pass on. I want to make sense out of this mess that is my life. I want to write my story, but I don't know where to start."

This letter led to offering workshops in prisons, churches, universities, and senior resource centers. Every class became an emotional experience as I grew to know and love these amazing people through their stories. I am less a teacher and more a coach and cheerleader. The stories are already there, my job is to inspire others to write and overcome the fear and doubt that every participant experiences regardless of past experiences, income, education, social status or even talent. Writing is a great equalizer. A prisoner, nun, or CEO of a major company each has a life story to tell and a unique voice. I wrote this book as a simple guide to help people write their life story. Your story is worth telling.

HOW TO USE THIS BOOK

This book is designed to use along with a journal you so you can jot down memories and do the exercises in short chunks of time. You can jump in anywhere, do the exercises, and start to write. If a section captures your interest, keep writing. If not, go on until you find a word association or question that pops out at you. Many of exercise are timed for three minutes, but you can write longer. Write freely without thinking about spelling, grammar or wondering if the writing is good. Give yourself the freedom to write drivel. Your goal is to keep your pen moving and not think about style or form. Brainstorm ideas by making lists of ideas, words, concepts, and images. Write whatever comes into your mind. Mind maps help you stay in your creative right brain and help you to see the interconnectedness of ideas. Simply circle a main idea in the center of a piece of paper. Using spokes, allow your mind to free associate supporting words and ideas. Sharing stories with others will spark more ideas.

THE BIG QUESTIONS

I always ask my students why they signed up for my memoir class. Some say that they have wanted to write for years and are finally making the commitment. Others were given family letters or photos and this prompted a vision of a memoir. Most students talk about passing on their stories before it's too late. So, I'll ask you, "Why are you reading this book?" Do you have a yearning to make sense out life? Do you want to explore how your family and early life experiences shaped you? Have you wondered what your life has added up to? These are not new questions. A human desire for authenticity and a yearning for wholeness have their roots in the beginning of human language and the philosophers of antiquity. Plotinus of Delphi said that there are only three universal concerns of humanity.

1. Who am I?

2. Why am I here?

3. What will become of me?

Thousands of years later, we are still asking these questions and searching for meaning. Reflecting and writing can help you grapple with the big questions of life. When you have found your voice and you know why you're writing and to whom, you'll be more motivated to stay on track. Ponder these big questions and relate them to memoir writing. Write these exercises in your journal. We will be returning to them again.

WHO AM I?

Who is the person writing this memoir? What experiences helped shape you? What circumstances led you down certain paths? Are you comfortable in your skin?

A mind map is an illustration that circles a main idea in a middle of the page with spokes representing supporting ideas. Write your full name in the middle of the page and circle it. Now cluster it with details, facts and reflections. Consider these points: Write about your birth. Were you named for someone or did your name have significance? Did you have a nickname? Did you like your name? Did you call yourself something else along the way? Was your name common? Is it a popular name today for new babies? Does it reflect your nationality? What words would describe your personality? Has it changed over time? Find a few pictures of yourself at various stages from early childhood to adulthood. Who is that person? Briefly describe yourself.

Write about your hidden self. What characteristics do you not want others to know? How do other people see you? What masks do you wear in certain situations or around certain people?

WHY AM I HERE?

Write about your purpose in writing this memoir. Is it to inform, educate, pass on stories, entertain, retrieve memories, heal trauma, or set the record straight? Is it to make sense out of your life? Do you want to save others from making mistakes? Do you want to express your love or pass on blessings? Do you want your great-greats to know what it was like to live on a farm at the turn of the century, cross the country in a wagon train, or live through the 60's? Do you want your grandchildren to appreciate the sacrifices of your parents and grandparents? Do have a slice of life that just must be told? Do you have a few lessons you really want to pass on? Are you trying to organize your photos, give shape to your memories, find out more about your ancestors, or figure out how you got here from there? Your reason may change as you continue to write. Write a few sentences about your purpose.

Write a few sentences about what you consider to be your purpose in life.

WHAT WILL BECOME OF ME?

First write about what will become of your story. To whom are you writing your memoir? Consider these questions: Is it directed to your children, grandchildren, nieces or nephews, friends, larger community or for yourself? Do you want to pass on lessons to living grandchildren or a great, great grandchild yet unborn? Do you want to get it published or is it just for yourself or your family? Can you envision someone picking this up 100 years from now? Who cares that you are writing? Briefly describe your audience.

Write a few sentences that reflect on what you think will become of you. What is your belief about life after death?

As you consider these three questions, think about what Carl Jung referred to as archetypes. They include images that cut across cultures, times, and religions. They often show up in dreams, fantasies, folklore and songs. They include The Wicked Stepmother, The Princess, The Hero, The Good Mother, The Victim, The Good Child, The Villain, and The Crone. Who in your life were examples of archetypes? What shows up in your dreams?

WHAT IS MEMOIR?

Over the years, I have taught classes with such titles as Legacy, Spiritual Autobiography and Memoir, but the goal was the same: writing stories about your life. I grew to like the concept of memoir because it speaks to the struggle to tease order out of meandering memories. The natural mind wanders, zigzags, and jumps around. This is why mind maps are so effective in writing. They create wholeness out of unconnected memories that pop up from nowhere. Memoir writing is creating a story out of the raw material of your life. Instead of just listing facts about an event, memoir ponders, struggles and strives to make sense out of the people and events that helped shape your life. It attempts to bring people and feelings to life. Memoir isn't neat and tidy. It asks you to dive in and start exploring that big family story that you can't shake or that event that changed the flow of your life. It may prod you to focus on writing letters or lessons that you've learned along the way. It weaves facts and reflection together. An autobiography usually starts at the beginning and is a lineal account of key transitions or turning points. Memoir plops you down in a certain period of your life where you can roam and meander and reflect. In short, memoir is a slice of life rather than a chronological record of all the major events of your life. It is a priceless gift that you give to not only loved ones and future generations but also to yourself.

THREE GIFTS

I'm going to wave my magic wand and give you three gifts:

1. *You have a unique voice and the ability to express yourself in writing.*
2. *You have something worthwhile to say.*
3. *Your story will be a blessing and a gift of love.*

These three gifts are wrapped brightly in your **willingness (see W)**.

M is for Memoir

"In the coming world, they will not ask me 'Why were you not Moses?' They will ask me: 'Why were you not Zusya?'"
-*Rabbi Zusya*

"The privilege of a lifetime is being who you are."
-*Joseph Campbell*

"Our essential purpose is to become the best version of ourselves."
-*Matthew Kelly*

"The true art of memory is the art of attention."
-*Samuel Johnson*

"Attention—Yes!
That's present! And present, you see, makes past and future."
-*Dalai Lama*

"The great danger for most of us is not that our aim is too high and we miss it, but that it is too low and we reach it."
-*Michelangelo*

"Whenever we children came to stay at my grandmother's house, we were put to sleep in the sewing room, a bleak, shabby, utilitarian rectangle, more office than bedroom, more attic than office, that played to the hierarchy of chambers the role of a poor relations. It was a room seldom entered by the other members of the family, seldom swept by the maid, a room without pride; the old sewing machine, some castoff chairs, a shade-less lamp, rolls of wrapping paper, piles of cardboard boxes that might someday come in handy, papers of pins, and remnants of material united with the iron folding cots put out for our use and the bard floor boards to give an impression of intense and ruthless temporality. Thin white spreads, of the kind used in hospitals and charity institutions, and naked blinds at the windows reminded us of our orphaned conditioned and of the ephemeral character of our visit; there was nothing here to encourage us to consider this our home."
-*Mary McCarthy,*

"It's not what you look at that matters. It's what you see."
-*Henry David Thoreau*

A

A is for **authentic**. Does your writing reflect who you are? It is easy to imitate the voice of another author or take on the tone of a person you admire. If it doesn't ring true, try a different approach. Find your authentic voice. Read your work out loud and see if it sounds like you. Listen to your unique tone as you talk and write from your authentic core. Pay attention to what goes on around you and within you. What are those thoughts and beliefs floating through your mind and how do they shape your world view?

A is for **awareness**. Be aware of your setting. Look around you. Now go back to when you were a child. Perhaps you were visiting your grandmother. What books were probably on the shelf? What was she wearing? Close your eyes and let this awareness settle in you. Also, be aware of the importance of writing. When you are tempted to scatter your energies, sit down and write. Be aware of how important your story is for you and for your reader. Imagine opening up an old desk and finding a secret drawer and in it is a letter of love by your great, great grandfather for his great, great grandchildren. Wouldn't you be thrilled? Is there anything more important today than writing your story? Write down the activities you are willing to give up or delegate so you can carve out writing time.

Advice: What have you learned that needs to be shared with the nextgeneration? Write about a valuable lesson that you want to pass on.

Write about a time when you felt **aware** of the beauty of life. Was it really looking at a flower, eating an orange, watching the sunset? Go. Three minutes.

Write about **archetypes**. What shows up in your dreams or fantasies?

Write about **anger**. Write about a situation that really upset you. Describe who was involved, what happened and why you felt such rage. Don't hold back.

"Man is what he believes."
-Anton Chekhov

"If you call forth that which is in you, it will save you. If you do not call forth what is in you, it will destroy you."
-Gospel of St. Thomas

"Stories have to be told or they die, and when they die; we can't remember who we are or why we're here."
-Sue Monk Kidd

"In September 1925, when I was just nine, I set out on the first great adventure of my life—boarding school...all Headmasters are giants, and this one was no exception...he gave me the kind of flashing grin a shark might give to a small fish just before he gobbles it up. The Headmaster moved away to another group and I was left standing there beside my brand-new trunk and my brand-new trunk box. I began to cry."
-Roald Dahl

"Spirit of the fountain; spirit of the garden,
Suffer us not to mock ourselves with falsehood
Teach us to care and not to care
Teach us to sit still even among these rocks,
Our peace in His will
And even among these rocks…"
-T.S. Eliot

"All human evil comes from this: a mans' being unable to sit still in a room."
-Blaise Pascal

B

B is for **beliefs**. What stories reflect your beliefs? They may include hard work, responsibility, honesty, faith, love, kindness or service. Where did you learn these beliefs? How have these beliefs changed? What spiritual beliefs have helped you in tough times and which ones were self-defeating??

B is for **believing**. Do you believe in yourself and your ability to write? Nurture that voice inside that says, "You can do this." Ignore that crazy voice that says, "You're wasting your time. What makes you think you can write?" You don't have to wait to be told that you have talent. You don't have to have a college degree or attend special workshops. Just get writing. Is there something you used to believe in that you don't anymore?

Birth: When and where were you born? Was there anything that was unique or different about your birth or infancy? Did you feel loved and wanted? Find a picture of yourself as a baby. See the innocence, the wholeness, the miracle of being. How did your birth order affect your life and relationship with your parents and siblings? Who really raised you if you were the youngest of a large family? Were you indulged and spoiled? Did you have a lot of responsibilities? Did you get a lot of attention or did you feel ignored and lost in the shuffle? Did you feel intense pressure to succeed?

Birthday: Pick a birthday that stands out. See the scene in rich detail. Who was there? Describe the cake, your clothes, house, furniture, toys, knick-knacks, books, and landscape that surrounded you. You may not remember the exact cake, but you know if your mom baked it or if she bought it at the bakery. What was typical? How do you celebrate now?

Belonging: Write about **belonging**. Did you feel part of a tribe? Did you feel a sense of belonging or were you different from your family? Go. Three minutes.

"If the water were clear enough,
If the water were still,
But the water is not clear,
The water is not still."
-*Stanley Kunitz*

"Man's mind, once stretched by a new idea, never regains its original dimensions."
-*Oliver Wendall Holmes*

"We shall not cease from
    exploration
And the end of all our
    exploring
Will be to arrive where we
    started
And know the place for the
    first time."
-*T.S. Eliot*

"When on some gilded cloud or flower, my gazing soul dwell an hour."
-*Wordsworth*

"There is no agony like bearing an untold story inside you."
-*Zora Neale Hurston*

"The beautiful rests on the foundations of the necessary."
-*Ralph Waldo Emerson*

C

C is for the **critical** inner voice that **creates** doubts and fear. Acknowledge your doubts and fears and move on. Tell your **critic** to take a nice long nap. What does this critical voice say to you? Ignore these voices and keep writing.

C is for **creativity**. Because the brain thinks in pictures and images, writing comes more naturally when you cluster ideas around a main point instead of writing in a linear way. Mind maps tap into your creative, free-flowing, natural style of writing. In just a few minutes, mapping creates a unified, coherent, interconnected cluster of words that reflects a sense of wholeness. Be concrete as you write quickly about a memory. Add details, describe scenes and get the words down. Don't worry about spelling or grammar. Later you can call upon the left side of your brain to edit, create structure, research facts, and look at sequence and style.

Childhood: Many people structure their memoir around their childhood since that is the foundation for the rest of their life. What are your first thoughts when you hear the word, childhood? Do pleasant thoughts come to mind? Do you take a deep breath and marvel that you survived? What color would you paint your childhood? (see appendix for more questions).

Commitment, completion and courage: Commit to completion. Commit to having the courage to tell your story. Write about these three big "C's."

Cars: Write about cars. Describe the car you rode in as a child. Write about your first trip? Do you remember falling asleep in the car? What are stories you heard about trips and your parent's car?

Christmas: What was this holiday like for you growing up? Did your family celebrate it or were you raised in a different religion or culture? If so, what was that like? How do you celebrate today?

"We are here to do.
And through doing to learn;
And through learning to know;
And through knowing to experience wonder;
And through wonder to attain wisdom;
And through wisdom to find simplicity;
And through simplicity to give attention;
And through attention
To see what needs to be done.
				-Ben Hei Hei

"If I had to select one quality one personal characteristic, that I regard as being most highly correlated with success, whatever the field, I would pick the trait of persistence. Determination—the will to endure to the end, to get knocked down seventy times and get up off the floor saying, 'Here comes number seventy-one!'"
				-Richard M. Devos

"We need people who understand darkness, and by their presence can hold us through to the light."
				-Richard Rohr

"To forget one's ancestors is to be a brook without a source, a tree without a root."
				-Chinese Proverb

"For a dream image to work in life
it must, like a mystery,
be experienced as fully real."
				-James Hillman

D is for **details**. One of the biggest questions that plagues every writer is how much detail to add. What do we select and what do we ignore? What are boring details and what is significant? Pour out every detail and write from your heart. Later you will edit with your head. For now, get your story down with as much detail as possible. Writing is the process. After you have picked out one memory write freely about the event. Add as many details as you can think of. If it helps, put this event or main idea in the center of a blank page. Memory clusters help you quickly get down all the details to create a unified whole. Use all your senses. What did you see, smell, hear, touch, taste? What would you likely be eating be around the dinner table? What would be the smells in the kitchen? What types of words and conversation would have likely been spoken? What kinds of clothes would people be wearing? What furniture surrounds the scene? What toy might be in the corner? What books are on the shelves? What magazines are on the coffee table? What music is playing on the radio? Jot down as many facts as you remember. For example, "We lived at 7280 Cade Road. The year was 1952."

D is for **decades**. Draw your illustration or take note cards and use one for each decade of your life. Quickly jot down everything that happened in that decade.

Discipline. Write when you don't feel like it or you think your writing is bad. Keep going even when you're discouraged. Writing a memoir can seem daunting. Write a one-page letter or make a list of lessons you want to pass on. Sketch out a memory map of your life or draw a river with major transitions.

Darkness: Write about a time when you could not see the beauty around you. The world was dark. You couldn't see a way out. How did you find your way?

Dreams. Write about dreams. Did you have a major dream?

M is for Memoir

"Because I have no time
To set my ladder up and climb
Out of the dung and straw
Green poems laid in a dark store
Wither and grow soft
Like unturned apples in a loft."

-Jon Stallworthy

"If your mind is empty, it is…open for anything. In the beginner's mind there are many possibilities, in the expert's there are few."

-Shunyu Suzu

"When everything else has gone from my brain—the President's name, the state capitals, the neighborhoods where I lived, and then my own name and what it was on earth I sought, and then at length the faces of my friends, and finally the faces of my family—when all this has dissolved, what will be left, I believe, is topology: the dreaming memory of land as it lay this way and that. I will see the city poured rolling down the mountain valleys like slag, and see the city lights sprinkled and curved around the hills' curves, rows of bonfires winding."

-Annie Dillard

"…and is indeed only a rather hazy impression. I am lying in a pram, in the shadow of a tree. It is a fine, warm summer day, the sky blue, and golden sunlight darting through the green leaves. The hood of the pram has been left up. I have just awakened to the glorious beauty of the day, and have a sense of indescribable well-being. I see the sun glittering throughout the leaves a blossom of the bushes. Everything is wholly wonderful, colorful and splendid."

-Carl Jung

Sharon K. Ferrett

E

E is for **earliest memory** Do a memory cluster of your earliest memory by putting the topic in the center of a page and circle it. Now brainstorm all supporting ideas. And cluster them around the main idea. Clusters may include: **Place**: in our farmhouse on Cade Road in rural Michigan. **People**: my mom is standing over me. **Surroundings**: my crib, my parent's bed against the wall, dresser, light coming in from the window. **Feelings**: contentment, happy, curious. **Weather**: outside it was late summer. **Clothes**: My mom may have been wearing a cotton housedress. **Time frame**: around 1946. **Larger world**: World War II had ended. **Smells**: Coffee brewing, bacon frying, toast, lilac bush blooming outside window, mothballs from closet. **Texture**: flannel sheets, my smooth skin, my mother's warm kiss, my dad's slightly scratchy face. **Sounds**: birds chirping, older brother playing, people bustling, newspaper rustling. **Color**: muted shades of blues, greens, faded covers, wallpaper with little pink roses.

E is for **excuses**. You don't need a better memory, more time, talent or a better writing space or tools. All you really need is a pen and paper and the willingness to write everywhere and anywhere. Get your story down. Jump in and see where your writing takes you. Write simple, direct and honest stories from the heart in your own words. Write about your experiences, thoughts, feelings and insights. You are the only person who can tell your story. You can do this. Face each excuse and move on. Write about an **intense experience** that made you feel alive.

E is for **empathy**. For example, instead of describing your mother coping with raising small children, imagine if you were in her shoes. What must it have been like for her? **Enter** into the body of your mother and write about how she moves, what she is wearing, her conversations and her tone.

Write about **envy**. How did you learn to **embrace** your talents instead of comparing them to others? When did you find your own voice?

"Avoiding danger is no safer in the long run than outright exposure. The fearful are caught as often as the bold."
-Helen Keller

"I will show you fear in a handful of dust."
-T.S. Eliot

"What is writing, if it is not the countenance of our daily experience: sensuous, contemplative, imaginary, what we see and hear, dream of, how it strikes us, how it comes into us, travels through us, and emerges in some language hopefully useful to others."
-M.C. Richards

"Don't start by trying to make the book chronological. Just take a period. Then try to remember it so clearly that you can see things: what colors and how warm or cold and how you got there. Then try to remember people. And then just tell what happened. It is important to tell what people looked like, how they walked, what they wore, what they ate. Put it all in. Don't try to organize it. And put in all the details you can remember. You will find that in a very short time things will begin coming back to you, you thought you had forgotten. Do it for very short periods at first but kind of think of it when you aren't doing it. Don't think back over what you have done. Don't think of literary form. Let it get out as it wants to. Over tell it in the matter of detail—cutting comes later. The form will develop in the telling."
-John Steinbeck

F

F is for **form**. At first, just start writing and allow the structure to form around your stories. Don't get hung up on definition. A letter may turn into a series of lessons or stories about your mother. Here are common themes that may help frame your memoir:

- Stages of life or ages (childhood, adolescent, college student, adult, elder)
- Decades or Historical eras (The Depression years, WWII, The 60's)
- Homes or Places lived (Growing up on a Farm in the Midwest)
- Travel (My year in Italy, lighthouses visited)
- Transitions (Marriage, divorce, moving, serious illness, death of loved ones)
- Family (children, parents, grandparents, family pets, and good friends)
- Religion, Spiritual Growth, Forgiveness
- Trauma (Abuse, depression, rape, prison, injury, war trauma, grief)
- Lessons Learned
- Nature and How It Shaped my Life
- Career, jobs, or roles (My Life as Mayor, Pastor's Wife, Caring for mom)

Write about **forgiveness**. Was there a **family feud** that caused hard feelings? What happened? Who was involved? What can't you forgive?

Facts: Memoir is a blend of fact and reflection. For example: **Fact**: My father was born in 1909 and came of age during the Great Depression. **Refection**: I think he was very self-reliant and thrifty because of his childhood experiences and losing his job in his 20's. He was a kind, moral and good man.

Friends: Jot down your first **friend**, your best **friends**, and your life-long pals for each life stage. What are the events with these friends that are most memorable?

"People deal too much with the negative, with what is wrong… Why not try and see positive things, to just touch those things and make them bloom?"
                                       -Thich Nhat Hanh

"You can't step into the same river twice."
                                       -Heraclitus

"When a bee stings, she dies. She cannot sting and live. When men sting, their better selves die. Every sting kills a better instinct. Men must not turn bees and kill themselves in stinging others."
                                       - Francis Bacon

"Do all the good you can,
By all the means you can,
In all the ways you can,
In all the places you can,
To all the people you can,
As long as ever you can."
                                       -John Wesley

"Growth is the only evidence of life."
                                       -Cardinal Newman

G

G is for **gratitude**. Thankfulness and appreciation for your relationships, for nature, good food and health can help create feelings of well-being and happiness. **Gratitude** is interconnected to praise, prayer, and meditation. Write about a time when you felt gratitude. Did this feeling make you want to be **generous** with others? Give thanks for the space you've created to focus on this opportunity. You get to write and you're **good enough**. You've been given a priceless **gift**. Pass it on. Don't let your story die. Now, pick up your pen.

G is for **gathering. Gather** photos, stories, and special objects such as your dad's watch, your grandmother's ring, or your aunt's quilt. Each time you hold them and reflect, you'll see something new or feel a new emotion.

Generosity: Write with a **generous** and open heart. You might find that what you thought you knew for sure, turns out to be wrong. What you thought was a fact turns out to be an opinion. With a generous heart, you can now see people with compassion. What was viewed as a catastrophic event may now highlight the **gifts of strength**, forgiveness, courage and resiliency. It's as if the past changes when looked at through the eyes of a lifetime of experiences. Maybe this is the time to awaken to the idea of possibilities. Perhaps open your mind to new ways of seeing. If the past isn't as we thought it was, maybe the present isn't either. Letting go of frozen beliefs, opinions and views is freeing. What would happen if you loved and forgave yourself completely? Writing can heal and transform. It can help sort out the things that **gnaw** at you.

Goals: What goals were your top priority? How did your goals impact your life? How did they impact your family? What goals do you still have?

"Call it a clan, call it a network, call it a tribe, call it a family. Whatever you call it, whoever you are, you need one."
-Jane Howard

"I expect I shall be a student to the end of my days."
-Anton Chekhov

"You must have a room, or a certain hour or so a day, where you don't know what was in the newspapers that morning, you don't know who your friends are, you don't know what you owe anybody, or what anybody owes to you. This is a place where you can simply experience and bring forth what you are and what you might be. This is the place of creative incubation."
-Joseph Campbell

"People who fail to achieve what they want in life don't want it badly enough to do the hard work. There just ain't no golden chariot that will take you there."
-Charles E. Wilson

"The used key is always bright."
-Benjamin Franklin

"A word is dead
When it is said
Some say.
I say it just
Begins to live
That day."

-Emily Dickinson

H is for **habit**. Make writing every day a habit. Choose an **hour** where you can sit quietly and write and reflect. Write about the power of habit.

Humanity. Write large. See the humanity in each person. See the **humanity and humor** in your family. What if you just accepted everyone and saw their worth?

H is for **handle** and asking, **"How about?"** How can you get a handle on this big project called your life? How about if you try and condense your memoir into a few short words: **One Word**: What is one word that would describe your family? **Song**: What is a song that would best describe your family? Your life? **Movie**: What is a movie that would best describe your family? **Book**: What is a book that would describe your family?

Three Word Memoir
Title your memoir in three words. Use lots of examples.
Examples:

> I Am Blessed
> Life is Good
> Finding My Voice
> 60: Now What?

Six Word Memoir
Title your memoir in six words.
Examples:

> I'm 80: Still a Rough Draft
> I'm 50: Still Blaming my Parents
> Forgiveness is the Key to Happiness
> Found my childhood sweetheart. Shouldn't have.

High school: Tell me about high school. Tell me about a day you wish had never **happened.**

> "Then from a remote part of his soul, from the past of his tired life, he heard a sound."
>
> *-Hermann Hesse*

> "Our lives may be determined less by our childhood than by the way we have learned to imagine our childhoods. We are...less damaged by the traumas of childhood than by the traumatic way we remember childhood as a time of unnecessary and externally caused calamities that wrongly shaped us."
>
> *-James Hillman*

> "So, with the lamps all put out, the moon sunk, and a thin rain drumming on the roof, a down pouring of immense darkness began. Nothing it seemed, could survive the flood, the profusion of darkness which, creeping in at keyholes and crevices, stole round window blinds, came into bedrooms, swallowed up her a jug and basin, there a bowl of red and yellow dahlias, there the sharp edges and firm bulk of a hest of drawers."
>
> *-Virginia Woolf*

> "Imagination is more important than knowledge."
>
> *-Albert Einstein*

> "Imagination is the Divine Body in every man."
>
> *-William Blake*

• •

I

I stands for **illustrations**. You may want to **illustrate** your life with a drawing of a river or use a life cycle spiral. Pinpoint on the river or life cycle where you are at this point in your life. This is your life. Let the impact of your wholeness sink in. You made it. Here you are now. Close your eyes and give thanks. Let your eyes go to an earlier time. Using your illustration, jot down the ten most important events and the year of the event. Write a few sentences describing what took place. Observe who was **involved** in these events. What decade was more eventful? Choose the top three events and write a paragraph or two.

Imagine. How do you imagine your memoir? **Imagination** can help you gain a sense of how your memoir might unfold. Can you see it completed? How have you imagined your childhood? Can you reframe it from a different perspective? What do you now give thanks for even though at the time the situation may have been difficult? What did you learn from this experience? Vivid imagination creates rich sensory visions and ideas come alive. Write about imagination.

I is for getting **involved** with other writers. As you listen to stories, your own memories will be sparked. A class can create structure, discipline, foster creative ideas and offer support, encouragement and camaraderie. You may feel more connected by common struggles and experiences and the universality of the most basic needs and desires. Becoming involved can ease the loneliness and isolation of writing. Sharing stories builds deep connections and are the voices of our common humanity. Your story is part of this link and only you can write it, but others can cheer, encourage and **inspire** you.

Ideals: Write about the ideals and principles that you value and want to pass on.

Inspiration. I went through a lot, but **I am here!**

"There is a track just waiting there for each of us, and once on it, doors will open that were not open before and would not open for anyone else. Everything does start clicking along and, yes, even Mother Nature herself supports the journey. I have found that you do have only to take that one step toward the gods and they will then take ten steps toward you."
-Joseph Campbell

"A journey of a thousand miles must begin with a single step."
-Lao Tzu

"The goal of the hero trip
down to the jewel point
is to find those levels in the psyche
that open, open, open,
and finally, open to the mystery
of your Self being
Buddha consciousness
Or the Christ.

That's the journey.

It is all about finding
That still point in your mind
Where commitment drops away."
-Joseph Campbell

J

J is for **Journey**. Where are the highlights? Look at your life cycle and pinpoint about a dozen or so of the most important life events, transitions or major changes that occurred on your journey. Write about when your life changed. It was flowing along and suddenly or gradually it changed direction and everything was different. What key event triggered the change? What road did you take that made a difference? What would have happened if you had taken another path or if an event had happened or not happened? What would have happened if you hadn't moved, your parents hadn't lost their home, your father had invested in more education, or you had married another? How did a choice hurl you down a path that was difficult to change? Did you turn down chances to be a better person? What doors were opened for you along your journey?

What key transitions, turning points or memorable happenings occurred during these stages:

- Birth to age five
- Age six to ten (elementary school)
- Eleven to thirteen (junior high)
- Fourteen to eighteen (high school)
- Nineteen to twenty-four (college/young adult)
- Twenty-five to twenty-nine (transition to adulthood)
- Thirty to forty (settling down)
- Forty-one to fifty-five (productive middle-years)
- Fifty-five to sixty-five (retirement)
- Sixty-six to seventy-one (post retirement)
- Seventy-two to eighty-five (early old-age)
- Eighty-six to ninety (old age)
- Ninety-one and beyond (really old age)

Write about **joy**. Write about a time when joy sprang from some deep part of you and you smiled or laughed. How do you express **joy**?

"…once you have flown, you will walk the earth with your eyes turned skyward for there you have been, there you long to return."
-*Leonardo Da Vinci*

"I am part of all that I have met."
-*Alfred Lord Tennyson*

"I shall pass through this world but once. If, therefore, there be any kindness I can show, or any good thing I can do, let me do it now; let me not defer it or neglect it, for I shall not pass this way again."
-*Etienne de Grellet*

"You have a soul in you of rare quality, an artist's nature; never let it starve for lack of what it needs."
-*Marcel Proust*

"Before you know what kindness really is
you must lose things,
feel the future dissolve in a moment
like salt in a weakened broth.
What you held in your hand,
What you counted and carefully saved,
All this must go so you know
How desolate the landscape can be
Between the regions of kindness."
-*Naomi Shihab Nye*

"Let the beauty we love be what we do. There are hundreds of ways to kneel and kiss the ground."
-*Rumi*

Sharon K. Ferrett

K

K is for **keep writing**. Keep you hand moving. Don't think; just write. If you get stuck, look around you and write about what you see or write about what you're thinking. Write about what you remember and don't remember.

K is for **knowing**. You know those times in life when you just know something is true. Claim that gift of knowing. What do you know for sure?

What would you like your twenty-year-old self to **know**? What would your 100-year-old self want you to know? Write each a letter.

Write about a time when you had the wind **knocked** out of you. Wow! When did it hit you? When did you feel as if you had stumbled upon the secret to life? That time when your head split open and you saw clarity. Colors were bright. You were glad to be alive. You woke up for just a minute. Wow. What was that thought? Something important came to you that you knew was true. What was it?

Kindness: Write about kindness. When did you realize it's value?

Does anyone really **know** you? What would you like to reveal before you die?

What makes you want to **kneel** down and give thanks?

Write about your first **kiss**. Tell me about kissing and making up. Write about **kissing** a new born.

The Kitchen Sink: Write about the kitchen sink or sketch the **kitchen** of your childhood. I have an early memory of waking up to see my dad having his coffee looking out the window over the kitchen sink while watching the sun come up. I also think of the many hours spent washing dishes with my mom.

"Life is not a problem to be solved, but a reality to be experienced."
                                         -Kierkegaard

"Where there is love, there is life."
                                    -Mohandas Gandhi

Humorist Sam Levinson wrote in a letter, "…to my grandchildren and children everywhere. Leaving you everything I have had in my lifetime: a good family, respect for learning, compassion for my fellowman, and some four-letter words for all occasions like help, give, care, feel and love."

"Life review is really nothing other than rewriting—or writing for the first time—the story of your life, or writing your life into stories. And without stories, there is no pattern no understanding, no art, and no character—merely habits, events passing before the eyes of an aimless observer, a life unreviewed, a life lost in the living of it. Correctly lost, I must quickly add, for the least reflected upon, most undigested life is very much worth living—and the purpose of life in earlier years is to live it. Knowing come later. Life review doesn't belong to earlier years. Memoirs, autobiography, and the deep investigations of long-term psychoanalysis probably should be touched before 60."
                                         -James Hillman

"Eye to eye, we are nearer but we truly enter each other's metaphysical immortal beings only through thought and forever only through utterly unselfish love. Self is infinitely lonely; Love is infinitely inclusive."
                                     -R. Buckmister Fuller

"Arduous struggles, envious rivalries, even betrayals come back with a new valance. They don't hurt as much. The musing may even make them amusing. The long illness, the wrong marriage, all the slings and arrows of outrage lose their fire and forget their aim…Is this a subtle hint that the soul is letting go of the weights it has been carrying, preparing to lift off more easily?"
                                         -James Hillman

L

L stands for **lessons**. What have you **learned**? You could focus your writing around **lessons** that you learned and want to pass on. What advice do you want to give? Think of your audience. Who will read your memoir? Think of someone picking up your memoir a hundred years from now. Write as if you are able to time travel back and talk to a few of your future ancestors. Read your work **aloud**. Think of talking with them around a campfire. There they are; your cherished great grandchildren or great, great nieces listening to every word. Keep it simple. Remember three points:

1. Tell them what happened. What event taught you a lesson?

2. Tell them how you felt. What thoughts and feelings were going on within you? Describe the struggle.

3. Tell them what you learned. What were the lessons you want to pass on? What is your best advice? What do you most regret? If you could time travel back, what is one day you would change?

Letters of love
Write a simple one-page letter to your spouse, children, grandchildren or a special child or friend in your life.

- What have I loved about this person?
- What qualities or special talents does this person have that I appreciate?
- Do I have a special memory of this person?
- What wishes and hopes do I have for this person?
- What lessons do I want to pass on?

Love: Tell me about love. Have you risk going deeper into love?

Loneliness: Write about a time in your life when you were lonely.

Life Review: Look with love on all your **life experiences** along your incredible journey. As you go through your life review, choose three challenging or hurtful events. With perspective maturity and time, do you see them differently? What do you now appreciate? With joy exclaim, "I did it. I survived. I am here!"

"Never say about anything, 'I have lost it', but only 'I have given it back.'
-Epictetus

"I am convinced that it is not the fear of death that haunts our sleep so much as the fear that our lives will not have mattered."
-Rabbi Harold Kushner

"The day is sufficient unto itself."
-Book of Mathew

"Anyone who has survived his childhood has enough information about life to last him the rest of his days."
-Flannery O'Connor

"To be a person is to have a good story to tell."
-Isak Dinsen

"This is the mother-love, which is one of the most moving and unforgettable memories of our lives, the mysterious root of all growth and change; the love that means homecoming, shelter, and the long silence from which everything begins and in which everything ends."
-Carl G. Jung

M

M is for **memories**. Choose a memory that pops out. Use a mind map as a way to visualize the details of this memory. Circle the main idea you are writing about and jot down memories, ideas and facts around this main idea. (Later you can check them as you do research.) Next, jot down images, questions, descriptions, and feelings that come up. Use reflection to ponder and speculate. Memoir is like a three-legged stool in that it is supported by memories, reflection, and facts. Write a memory of your **mother** and do a mind map. For example:

Memory of your Mother
I have this image of my mother in the garden. I think she is picking strawberries or flowers. I can see her bending over and putting them in a basket. She's wearing a printed cotton housedress. The sun is shining through the trees, but it is hot. She has on a straw hat over her tight grey curls.

Facts
- Velma Mary Hollenbeck
- Born July 23, 1910 in Imlay City, Michigan at her mother's home
- The family included her fraternal twin, Thelma, her sister, Beulah, was three years older and brother, Noble, was five years younger
- She married and had six children

It must have been difficult for my **mom** to juggle raising a large family and work alongside of my dad on the farm. She did all the housework, without modern conveniences, canned from her large garden, and milked cows. It seemed she was happiest when she was outside in the fields or garden. She was a hard worker.

Hazy memory. I know some people who when they open the front door of their childhood, small details come rushing forth. They remember vivid scenes. I can't. Much of my childhood is a black space. So, I come at my writing from the side door. I jot down wispy memories, list facts, ponder events, reflect on scenes and situations and sit myself down everyday and write.

Write about **mistakes**. Write about what has been **on your mind**. What wakes you up at night or **early morning?**

> "Our fears are more numerous than our dangers, and we suffer more in our imagination than in reality."
> -*Seneca*

> "After the game, the king and pawn go into the same box."
> -*Italian Proverb*

> "The only real voyage of discovery consists not in seeking new landscapes but in having new eyes."
> -*Marcel Proust*

> "Give sorrow words…"
> -*William Shakespeare*

> "Do I contradict myself? Very well, then I contradict myself. I am large; I contain multitudes."
> -*Walt Whitman*

N is for **notice**. Look at pictures and notice the details. Now close your eyes and think about your childhood. How were people dressed, what did you eat, what books were in your shelves, what toys were in the toy box, what smells were coming out of the kitchen? Notice what wasn't said over the years. Was the big family story hushed? Did your dad not talk about the War? What is your BIG family story? Did your parents lose their jobs during the Great Depression? Did your aunt have a child out of wedlock and gave it up for adoption? Was someone murdered in the family? What secrets were kept in your family?

N is for **name**. Your name is your identity. What does your name mean to you? What significance does it have? Does it reflect your nationality or were you named after an ancestor? Did you have a nickname? Did you alter or change your name? Why? Tell me about your name.

N also stands for **"not going there"**. What story do you have trouble facing because the truth is too painful? Go for 3 minutes.

Note cards are a great way to organize. Using one note card for each decade of your life, do a memory cluster. Go three minutes.

Normal. Write about what was **normal** for your family and what wasn't.

In your journal or on the back of each **note card**, write sentences about the decade using only three words.

> Reading saved me
> I survived
> An invisible child
> The best years of my life
> The youngest child
> Married, but alone

"I must create a system, or be enslaved by another man's."
-William Blake

"Every child is an artist. The problem is how to remain an artist once he grows up."
-Pablo Picasso

"All thought is a feat of association; having what's in front of you bring up something in your mind that you almost didn't know you knew."
-Robert Frost

"Clear a space for the writing voice…you cannot will this to happen. It is a matter of persistence and faith and hard work. So, you might as well just go ahead and get started."
-Anne Lamott

"Sundays too my father got up early
and put his clothes on in the blue black cold,
then with cracked hands that ached
from labor in the weekday weather made
banked fires blaze. No one ever thanked him.

I'd wake and hear the cold splintering, breaking.
When the rooms were warm, he'd call,
and slowly I would rise and dress,
fearing the chronic angers of that house,

Speaking indifferently to him,
who had driven out the cold
and polished my good shoes as well.
What did I know, what didn't I know
of love's austere and lonely offices?"
-Robert Hayden

O

O is for order. You simply must bring organization to your photos, memories, stories, research, dates, specific incidents, experiences, etc. You can organize into piles with post it notes. You can **outline** your memoir.

O is for **order of birth**. Write about your birth order and how it influenced you. Were you the firstborn, youngest or middle? Were you an only child or one of many? Did you have a lot of responsibilities or were you babied and care-free? How was your childhood effected by your order of birth?

Observe everything and everyone. Observe the wonder of nature. Feel the sunlight, notice the texture, color, and smell of a flower, the shades of green and the birds and insects. Close your eyes and listen to sounds. Notice how people walk, their expressions, clothes, and speech. Listen to conversations. How do people talk in everyday language? Use your imagination to make up stories about people you observe. When you get stuck, just write about what you're observing.

Ordinary: What is ordinary about your life? Describe an ordinary day growing up. What do you love most about simple, ordinary days?

Finish the sentence, **Once upon a time**_____. For example,
As a little girl, I longed for companionship and wanted to belong. I was ignored, dismissed and desperately lonely. I learned to become best friends with myself and find comfort, peace, and adventure in books.

A class participant wrote:
Once upon a time there was a little girl who watched helplessly as three men in white jackets came and dragged her mommy away in a white truck with bars on the window. She noticed her mom was crying and the little girl was filled with rage and haunted by the men in white. Her dad and relatives ignored her questions and her broken heart. She wanted to feel included in the sadness. It took many years of struggle

and understanding for her to forgive her mother for going away to a mental hospital and for not saying goodbye. Her anguish was slowly replaced with compassion, love and gratitude.

Write about **opinions** you have. How were they formed?

"Great minds have purposes; others have wishes."
-Washington Irving

"The secret of success is constancy of purpose."
-Benjamin Disraeli

"Persistence. Nothing in the world can take the place of persistence.
Talent will not; nothing is more common than unsuccessful men with talent. Genius will not; unrewarded genius is almost a proverb. Education will not; the world is full of educated derelicts. Persistence and determination alone are omnipotent. The slogan 'Press on' has solved and always will solve the problems of the human race."
-Calvin Coolidge

"It's hard to beat a person who never gives up."
-Babe Ruth

"Men are disturbed not by things that happen, but by their opinions of the things that happen."
-Epictetus

P

P is for **parents**. The relationship between parent and child is primal and sets the stage and pattern for all other relationships. Who were these people? Did you know your parents as real people or just by the roles they played? Did you have heart-to-heart talks or enjoy just being together?

Ponder. Ask questions. Wonder. Reflect. Let your imagination fill in what you can't remember about clothes, food, the surroundings, and dialogue. What might have happened? What might everyone be wearing? What smells and textures might you have experienced? Keep your pen moving. You want to stay in the right brain. Don't think, just write. Then sit back and be curious about your life.

Photos: Pictures can help you remember scenes and events from various stages of your life. Who was this child? What personality traits were evident even then?

Purpose: Who will someday read this book? Feel their **presence**. Feel the presence of all your dear ones who have gone on before. What are they saying to you?

Pleasure: Do a mind map and jot down all the pleasures in your life. Simple. Big. Delightful. Where does your bliss lead? How have they changed since you were a kid? What is a perfect, pleasurable day? How would it start and end?

Patterns: Tell me about themes or patterns that seem to be coming up again and again as you write. Is there a period of time when a lot of events occurred? Do they cluster around a certain age? Where and when did they occur? This theme can help you determine shape and order for your memoir. For example, you may have several memories around school or your mother may be a common thread that runs through your writing.

Plot: If your life were a movie or book, what would be the plot? Let say you created a series of stories from your memories of childhood. How did you escape your emotionally abusive and overbearing mother? How did you get through the loss of your parents in your early 20's? What drives you to excel? What question or thread pulls your readers along; wanting to know more?

Write about **persistence and patience**. Were you ever **poor**? Explain.

> "I wish that life should not be cheap but sacred. I wish the days to be as centuries, loaded, fragrant."
> -Ralph Waldo Emerson

> "The important thing is not to stop questioning."
> -Albert Einstein

> "Be patient toward all that is unresolved in your heart, and try to love the questions themselves. Do not seek the answers that cannot be given you, because you would not be able to live with them, and the point is to live everything. Live the questions new. Perhaps you will gradually, without noticing it, live along some distant day into the answers."
> -Rainer Maria Rilke

> "When the inner and the outer are wedded, revelation occurs."
> -Hildegard of Bingen

> "Perceive that you are not yet begottoen, that yuu are in the womb, that you are young, that you are old, that you have died, that you are in the world beyond the grave. Grasp in your mind all this at once, all times and places, all substances and qualities and magnitudes together. Then you can begin to see with the way of the divine."
> -Hermes Trismegistus

Sharon K. Ferrett

Q

Q is for **questions**. When I started writing my memoir I had a lot of questions and few answers—and many, many regrets. Why had I not talked with my parents more or my aunts? I realized that I had to work with what I had and not look back. The questions served an important role in helping to shape my memoir and for helping others to write. When a question pops up, write it down and don't worry about the answer. You might reflect on what might have happened or ponder different outcomes. This is an important part of memoir. Use your imagination to speculate. Questions also spur conversation with others. An important question to ask is, "What major transitions or turning points occurred during each decade of my life?" What questions remain unanswered?

If you could talk with a departed loved one for one hour, what **questions** would you ask? What questions would you ask your 100-year-old sage self? In quiet, listen to the response.

Q is for **quick**. The three minute exercises are designed to get you writing in short burst of energy. You can always go back and add more, but there is value in timed writing. Are you quick to build bridges and take down walls or are you **quick** to take offense and build walls? Go three minutes.

Write about **quiet**. Was your home a **quiet** place? What is **silence to you?**

Tell me about **quitting**. What memory comes up? What can you give up easily?

Quilt: What does that word bring up? Did you have quilters in your family? Do you have a treasured **quilt**? Did you learn to sew or bake? Did you learn to do woodworking? What do you like to do with your hands?

What **qualities** define you? How were they developed? What qualities do you value in others?

"Life changes fast.
Life changes in the instant.
You sit down to dinner and life as you know it ends.
The question of self-pity.

Those were the first words I wrote after it happened."
          -Joan Didion

"I have ever thought religion a concern purely between our God and our conscience, for which we were accountable to Him, and not the priests. I have never told my own religion, nor scrutinized that of another. I never attempted to make a convert, nor wished to change another's creed. I have ever judged of the religion of others by their lives…For it is in our lives, not from our words, that our religion must be read."
         -Thomas Jefferson

"There are only two ways to live your life. One is as though nothing is a miracle. The other is as though everything is a miracle."
          -Albert Einstein

"We can make our minds so like still water that beings gather around us, that they may see their own images, and so live for a moment with a clearer perhaps even a fiercer life because of our quiet."
         -William Butler Yeats

R

R is for **remembering**. Circle I Remember as your main idea and surround it with memory clusters. "I remember my ninth birthday party, I remember our family vacations to the lake, I remember when my sister got in trouble, I remember when I almost drowned and so on." Write quickly. Go three minutes.

Room. Virginia Wolf spoke of a woman's need for a room of her own. Do you have a room of your own to write and reflect? Find a quiet space and review what you wrote. You may find memories underneath memories. Is there one memory that stands out? Circle it and develop it with clusters of detail. Spend time writing about what you remember. Write about a room of significance in your life. Where was your place of solace, peace and safety as a child?

Review and reflect on your life journey. You may want to write as an elder looking back. What sage advice would you give to your younger self?

R is for **research and reading**. You can talk with living relatives, go to libraries, church and township records, courthouses, and online to research dates, place of birth, etc. Read widely. Read a variety of memoirs and especially note those that are similar to your experiences. If you want to be a good writer, you have to read a lot and write a lot. Reject nothing. Read. Reflect. Write.

Red: Write about the color red or one event that reminds you of the color red. Go three minutes. For example, *"My mom had a pair of red heels. This was out of character for her as she was a farm wife and very practical. I thought she looked glamorous in these elegant red shoes. Someday, I'd have a pair of red shoes."*

Resilience: What helped you through this dark time? Who gave you a hand? What qualities helped you bounce back? Describe your strength.

Religion: Tell me about religion. What effect has it had on your life? Tell me about your spiritual life. Have you had a revelation or a spiritual experience?

> "Recognizing the sacred begins, quite simply, when we are interested in every detail of our lives."
> -*Chogyam Trungpa*

> "The last thing one knows is what to put first."
> -*Blaise Pascal*

> "Oh, for a life of sensations rather than of thoughts!"
> -*John Keats*

> "It is like fishing. But I do not wait very long, for there is always a nibble—and this is where receptivity comes in. To get started, I will accept anything that occurs to me. Something always occurs, of course, to any of us. We can't keep from thinking."
> -*William Stafford*

> "To write simply is as difficult as to be good."
> -*William Somerset Maugham*

> "Wherever men have lived there is a story to be told."
> -*Henry David Thoreau*

> "All suffering is bearable if it is seen as part of a story."
> -*Isak Dinesen*

S is for **start**. You don't need to have your memoir all laid out, or know the approach you're going to take. Just keep your pen moving quickly. Be creative and open yourself to new ideas and approaches. When you don't have a lot of facts or stories, **speculate** on what could have happened given a certain time, place and circumstance. Write a **scene** about your story.

S is for **sensations**. What sensations create memories? What smells, textures, sounds, taste, sights, remind you of your childhood? (Cinnamon, lilacs, Vicks vapor rub, or vanilla). What memory stands out? Be **specific**. Buick, not car. Red heels, not shoes. Old Spice, not aftershave. Oatmeal raison, not cookies.

Structure: You may be concerned because you don't know how to **structure** your writing. Just get your story down. Don't jump ahead and worry about where your writing is going. Write every day. Trust the process. As you answer questions and blend memories, facts and reflection, form will emerge.

Sayings: What bits wisdom or sayings or quotes might you have heard when you were young? For example: "A penny saved is a penny earned."

Secrets: What secret or shadowing part of your life have you avoided facing, writing or talking about? What stories will you never tell? How would telling a story rock the boat? Who would be hurt or might be embarrassed?

Singing: Write about an early memory of singing. When was the last time you really sang your heart out? How important is music in your life? Listen to old songs and see what images arise. If your family were a song, what would it be?

Sunday dinner: Write about a typical Sunday Dinner from your childhood.

Write about **suffering**. What did it teach you? Write about the sacred.

"What would happen if one woman told the truth about her life? The world would split open."
-*Muriel Rukeyser*

"Facts and truth really don't have much to do with each other."
-*William Faulkner*

"We must be true inside, true to ourselves, before we can know a truth that is outside us. But we make ourselves true inside by manifesting the truth as we see it."
-*Thomas Merton*

"Tell all the Truth but tell it slant—
Success in Circuit lies
Too bright for our infirm Delight
The Truth's superb surprise
As Lightening to the Children eased
With explanation kind
The Truth must dazzle gradually
Or every man be blind—"
-*Emily Dickinson*

"Few delights can equal the mere presence of one whom we trust utterly."
-*George MacDonald*

"What is true for you in your private heart is true for all men."
-*Ralph Waldo Emerson*

"Everyone has the right to tell the truth about her own life."
-*E. Bass and L. Davis*

T

T is for **truth**. A memoir is non-fiction so tell your story as truthfully as you can. Memory, however, is selective and writing is based on viewpoint, context and environment. Your recollection will, no doubt, be different from others who may have experienced the same event. When you avoid or deny, you obscure the truth; you block memory. Write your story. Raw. Don't try to pretty it up. Have you put off writing because you don't know if your memories are accurate or you worry that some stories shouldn't be told? How would telling a story rock the boat or cause hurt or embarrassment? Trust yourself. Build a tolerance for fear.

T is for **theme**. Is there a theme to your memoir? Caring for an elderly parent, travel, relationships, forgiveness, food, animals or the year of coping with a major loss. The point of your memoir is you. Let your experience speak.

T is for **title**. In a short sentence, write a possible title for your memoir. You might want to consider how you got from there to here? Write the first thoughts that comes to mind. For example:

- *Survivor: My Brush with Death*
- *Life on the Highways: Spiritual Lessons along the Way*
- *From the Ghettos to the Suburbs*
- *From Texas Wildfires to Kansas Tornados*

Treasures: Choose a ring, broach, compass, watch or necklace or some treasure that has a lot of meaning to you. Write about why it has personal value?

Trust: Write about trust and betrayal? Who do you **trust?**

Time: A major excuse for not writing is **lack of time**. Use small chunks of time that you have throughout the day. In three minutes, you can complete a mind map or write a paragraph. Write about the **passage of**

time and the times you were alone or suffered loss. What have you waited a **long time** for?

What **traditions** were most important? What couldn't be changed? Were there certain foods that had to be included at holidays? Write about traditions.

> "We shall not cease from exploration
> And the end of all our exploring
> Will be to arrive where we started
> And know the place for
> The first time."
>   *-T.S. Eliot*

> "Of course, there is no formula for success except, perhaps, an unconditional acceptance of life and what it brings."
>   *-Arthur Rubinstein*

> "I am an experiment on the part of nature,
> a gamble within the unknown,
> perhaps for a new purpose, perhaps for nothing,
> and my only task is to allow this game
> on the part of the primeval depths to take its course,
> to fulfill its will within me
> and make it wholly mine."
>   *-Herman Hesse*

> "You do not have to be good.
> You do not have to walk on your knees
> For a hundred miles through the desert, repenting.
> You only have to let the soft animal of your body
> Love what it loves...
>
> Whoever you are, no matter how lonely,
> The world offers itself to your imagination,
> Calls to you like the wild geese, harsh and exciting—
> Over and over announcing your place
> In the family of things."
>   *-Mary Oliver*

U is for **understanding**. One benefit of writing your life story is that you start to understand more about yourself, your parents, siblings, friends, and life. Reflect on the most challenging event in your life in which you were tested. List facts, dates, locations, people involved. How long did it last? Write your reflections. What did you learn from it? How did you survive? How did you overcome fear? Do you feel you are a stronger person because of it? For some the Great Depression was the most challenging event. For others being in a war, dealing with a major illness, losing a job, divorce, death in the family.

Write about your most challenging year and what you learned about life. Did you have one tremendous challenge or a series of smaller transitions that created a cumulative effect? How were you tested? Did you gain personal insight, become more resilient, learned perseverance, or gained strength. Did you feel as if you triumphed over a devastating situation and made the best of it? Write about how it felt when you were going through it and how you feel about it now. How has your perspective changed? Imagine going up to the 12th floor and viewing the event as a long parade in your life. Do you see it differently now? Was it part of your emotional or spiritual growth?

Who are you? Be clear, transparent, objective and **unbiased**.

What will become of you? What will become of your story? What is your legacy? Will your life be more than a dash between your birth and death?

What is **unusual** about your life? What choices did you make that were out of step with your time or family? What three qualities make you smarter than your IQ, your education level or your ability to take tests? (For example, I grew up on a farm and this experience is in my blood, bone and heart. The ability to work hard, resiliency and optimism are three qualities that have helped me be more successful and to survive life's rough patches.) What makes you **unique?** What are your strengths? Have you made friends with your shadows? Own it all!

"All that we are arises with our thoughts."
                                        -Buddha

"I know the way of all things by what is within me"
                                        -Lao Tzu

"There is a vitality, a life force, a quickening that is translated through you into action, and because there is only one of you in all time, the expression is unique. And if you block it, it will never exist through any other medium...and be lost. The world will not have it. It is not your business to determine how good it is nor how valuable it is; nor how it compares with other expressions. It is your business to keep it yours clearly and directly, to keep the channel open. You do not even have to believe in yourself or your work. You have to keep open and aware directly to the urges that motivate YOU. Keep the channel open. No artist is pleased. There is no satisfaction whatever at any time. There is only a queer, divine dissatisfaction; a blessed unrest that keeps us marching and makes us more alive."
                                        -Dancer Martha Graham

"When we were little, we had no difficulty sounding the way we felt; thus, most little children speak and write with real voice."
                                        -Peter Elbow

"When a woman speaks her truth, fires up her intention and feeling, stays tight with the instinctive nature, she is singing, she is living in the wild breath-stream of the soul."
                                        -Clarissa Pinkola Estes

"It is not enough to possess virtue as if it were an art. It should be practiced."
                                        -Cicero

V

V is for **visualize**. Visualize your memoir. Use all your senses to clearly see your project finished. Visualize yourself at different stages in your life. Do you use all your senses to remember? Go back over one of your I Remember memories (see R). Drench yourself in your senses. Write about sights, color, smells, tastes, sounds, and textures. Think about the sayings and conversations that might have been said. Collect photos, letters, objects, look at old magazines and books. Go back to your hometown. Walk the streets and fields. Talk with family and neighbors. Steep yourself in that time and place. What pops out?

Vivid Memory
A. Look at your life cycle and choose a slice of your life where a **vivid memory** pops out.

B. Use one full page for your memory cluster. Add details. Go three minutes.

C. Now write a story. Go ten minutes.

Vague. Don't fret if you have vague memories of your childhood. Some people can remember conversations and detailed events from childhood. Most of us don't. Stay with it. Tug at that sticky door that holds your memory. When you least expect it, out will slide details. You will smile with wonder. Dance around with that wispy, vague image until it begins to sway with you. Write about a vague memory that became clearer when you saw photos.

Vacations: Describe a vacation or outing you had with your family. What was unusual about your vacations? What were simple pleasures you enjoyed?

Vice. Write about a secret **vice** you had.

"Wild Nights—Wild Nights!
Were I with thee
Wild Nights should be
Our luxury!
Futile—the Winds—
To a Heart in port—
Done with the Compass—
Done with the Chart!
Rowing in Eden—
Ah, the Sea!
Might I but moor—Tonight—
In Thee!

      -Emily Dickinson

"There is not a moment when I do not feel the presence of a Witness whose eye misses nothing and with whom I strive to keep in tune."

      -Mahatma Gandhi

"If you bring forth what is within you, what is within you will save you."

      -Jesus

"There are voices which we hear in solitude, but they grow faint and inaudible as we enter into the world."

      -Ralph Waldo Emerson

"To wonder is to live in the world of novelty rather than law (or habit), of delight rather than obligation, and of the present rather than the future. Wonder requires a relaxed attitude, receptivity, an intuitive sense, a delight in juxtaposing and savoring particulars, sensuousness, openness, and participation."

      -Sam Keen

"Who is it that can make muddy water clear? No one. But left to stand, it will gradually clear of itself."

      -Lao-Tzu

W is for the **larger world**. Take a broader, more generous view. What was going on in your family at that time? Was your older sister pregnant or your grandfather dying? What was going on in the community at that time? Was there a disagreement with neighbors or a murder in a nearby city? What was going on in the larger world? Who was President of the United States? Was there a war going on? How did that affect everyone in your scene? What is going on within you as you related to the larger world? For now, speculate. Wonder.

W is for **wonder**. Be curious. Ask lots of questions and ponder what might have been going on. What questions kept going on in your head? Who, What, Where, When, How, Why? Think of the people who were involved, the place and what you were thinking and feeling. What feelings, motivations, and thoughts were going on within you? What did you know intuitively that no one would believe or listen to? Tune into the general mood and tone of the event.

W is for **wisdom**. What would your older self share with your younger self? What wisdom would you pass on? In one page, what have you learned?

W is for **willingness** which is the foundation and only requirement to writing. Be willing to do the exercises in this book. Be willing to be a bad writer knowing that with practice you'll be a good writer. Be willing to fail. Be willing to be the fool. Be willing to sit and write every day. Be willing to share some of your stories. Be willing to a beginner. Be that small child filled with wonder and delight. Be willing to have fun and feel gratitude that you have this opportunity.

Who Cares? Writing is a way to make sense and find meaning in your journey. Your story explores how you got to where you are and what it all means. It is a way to heal trauma and conflict and honor your inner life. You write to know yourself. Writing will transform you and inspire others in ways you cannot imagine. Some people stop writing because they hear a voice saying, "Your life's not interesting." Trust me, no one will be bored as they read about how you lived in a particular time and place. I care. I want to read your memoir. Keep writing.

Write about the **worst** day of your life. What does it whisper to you?

Wholeness: What activities make you feel whole?

What was outside your childhood **window?**

> "I exist as I am, that is enough,
> If no other in the world be aware I sit content,
> And if each and all be aware I sit content.
> One world is aware, and by far the largest to me, and that is myself,
> And whether I come to my own today or in ten thousand or ten million years,
> I can cheerfully take it now, or with equal cheerfulness I can wait."
> *-Walt Whitman*

> "If only, most lovely of all, I yield myself and am borrowed
> By the fine, fine wind that takes its course through the chaos of the world…"
> *-D.H. Lawrence*

> "Be helpless, dumbfounded,
> unable to say yes or no.
> Then a stretcher will come from grace
> To gather us up."
> *-Rumi*

X

X is for **eXcuses**. You may have started off with a bang—especially if you're taking a class or are in a writing group. You were excited, determined to write and gave it a big push. Where are you now? Let's check in. Are you writing everyday? You may find that life gets in the way and writing takes a back seat to daily busyness. Irrational thoughts tug at your good intentions. "I'm too cold or warm or hungry or tired. I need a nap or I need to clean the kitchen or flea comb the cat." Observe what is going on in your mind that keeps you from writing. What are the distractions? Are doubts slowly creeping into your once inspired mind? Do you wonder why you ever thought you could write? Do you fret about style and structure? Do you worry that you don't have a theme or sometimes can't even find the right words? Do you read something you've just written and say, "This is slop! No one will want to read this." These thoughts are not original. Every writer has doubts and worries that writing is a waste of time. Give your critic a cookie and send it out to play (that voice needs to lighten up). Quiet your chattering mind with routine, discipline, and observation. **When you get stuck, just write what you're observing.** Write about starts and stops. What excuses keep you from writing and what gets you started again?

X is for **don't cross out**. Don't worry about spelling, punctuation, or grammar. Just keep writing. You can edit later.

X also stands for **eXperiement**. Leap from one image to another. Play different music. Cook a meal your mom would have cooked. What images come up? Watch old movies. Read childhood books. Go back to your hometown. Talk with relatives and elders in the community. Take in landscapes while driving. What do these images bring up for you? Be creative. If you can't get there through the front door, go through the back or side doors. Write about a memory that seemed to come from nowhere.

Expressing. Writing is about finding your voice, **expressing** yourself, and allowing yourself the freedom to get it wrong or make a dozen attempts. Don't crumple up pages and throw them away. **Cross nothing out.** Save it. Try again. Write about a time when you felt silenced or when you felt you couldn't honestly express yourself.

> "If only, most lovely of all, I yield myself and am borrowed by the fine, fine wind that takes its course through the chaos of the world…"
>
> *-D. H. Lawrence*

> "I sometimes begin a drawing with no preconceived problem to solve, with only the desire to use pencil on paper and make lines, tones, and shapes with no conscious aim; but as my mind takes in what is so produced, a point arrives where some idea crystallizes, and then a control and ordering begins to take place."
>
> *-Henry Moore*

> "The most enviable writers are those who, quite often unanalytically and unconsciously, have realized that there are different facets to their nature and are able to live and work with now one, now another, in the ascendant."
>
> *-Dorothea Brande*

> "In my own experience, nothing is harder for the developing writer than overcoming his anxiety that he is fooling himself and cheating or embarrassing his family and friends. To most people, even those who don't read much, there is something special and vaguely magical about writing and it is not easy for them to believe that someone they know—someone quite ordinary in many respects—can really do it."
>
> *-John Gardner*

Y

Y is for **yearning**. There is a deep yearning to belong. Did you yearn to have a best friend? Did you yearn to be popular in school? Who were your first friends, best friends and lifelong friends? Did you yearn to have a closer relationship with your siblings or parents? We also yearn to make sense out of life. The short poem by Portia condenses life's lessons in five short paragraphs. What poem, book or movie helped you to make sense out of your life?

Write about **yearning**. What does your soul deeply **yearn** for?

Y is for **youth**. What did you do in your youth that you regret doing or not doing? Describe a typical youthful night out. Did you go to prom? Describe your youth. What did you look like, what was your personality? What are three lessons would you pass on to the young?

Learn to **yield** to new directions. You'll find that you may start with an idea and it changes naturally. Yield to that intuition. Tell me about your experience.

You. Does anyone really know **you?**

Yellow. Write about the color **yellow.**

Yes. Write about the word **"yes"**. Do you say, **"Yes"** to life?

Draw a mind map about **yes** or about **you.**
Example:

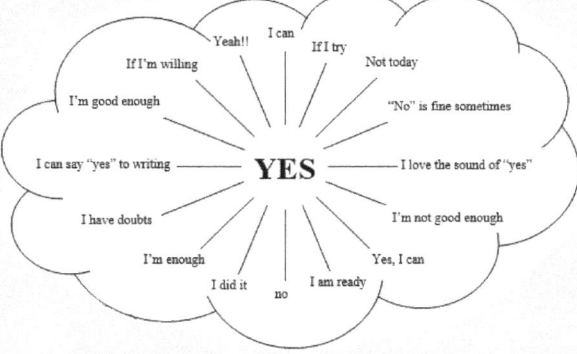

"there are two
kinds of human
beings in the world
so, my observation
has told me
namely and to wit
as follows
firstly
those who
even though they
were to reveal
the secret of the universe
to you would fail
to impress you
with any sense
of the importance
of the news
and secondly
those who could
communicate to you
that they had
just purchased
ten cents worth
of paper napkins
and make you
thrill and vibrate
with the intelligence
alter-ego"

-Don Marquis

"For the unlearned, old age is winter; for the learned, it is the season of the harvest."

-Hasidic Proverb

"Sleep is the golden chain that ties health and our bodies together."
-Thomas Dekker

Z

Z is for **zest**. When you have zest in your life, you feel as though the planets have lined up and you are in your zone.

Write about a time when the universe supported you. Doors opened and events came together to create results. Life flowed. How can you help the universe right now? How can you get into your **zone**? Go for 3 minutes.

ZZZZZZZZ. That sleepy time when you seem to be coasting, feel tired, bogged down or just in a fog. Be physical. Even if you usually use your computer for writing, carry a notebook so you can jot down memories and images throughout the day. Writing by hand connects to the heart and you tap different images. Writing is physical. As you walk, feel your physical body. Think of how it felt as a child or teenager. How will it feel as a 95-year-old? If you're writing about your grandfather as an old man, try walking like him.

Zig Zag: Memoir Zigs and zags. Don't worry about where to start or how to structure your writing. Jump in and allow your writing to flow.

Zap: The biggest fear most people have about writing is that they don't have talent or they are not good enough. Remember my magic wand? You were **zapped with magic**. You're good enough. Writing is a craft that improves with practice, patience, persistence, and discipline. Keep the energy going by writing in small chunks of time. Do memory clusters. Don't think about how you'll structure them or how to get published. Don't worry that they're scattered or think about which ones are important, which ones you'll use and which ones you'll set aside. Worry is another distraction. Stay in the present moment. Write about being **zapped** with a sense of confidence. You just knew that you were good enough to handle the task at hand. That deep knowing carried you through the inner critic of doubt, the fear, and the slips and slides and steps backward and forward. How did you ignore the inner critic? You are enough!

Sharon K. Ferrett

APPENDIX

Notes and Worksheets

This section will give you more questions,
exercises, worksheets, and an overview of the stages of life

EXERCISES

MOUNTAIN TOP

Under letter I, you were asked to draw an illustration of your life. Your illustration may be a river or a spiral illustrating your life cycle. Mark significant turning points or transitions. Choose one of these events and write about it for three minutes. Now imagine going to the top of a mountain and look down at your illustration. You now have distance, time, space, and a new perspective. Look down with a generous heart that is filled with love and compassion. You are objective, curious, and unattached. You take all this in as if you are watching the event as an interesting scene in a movie. Write about the lessons you learned. Write with appreciation and gratitude for the whole of your life.

FIRST MEMORY

Go backwards in your childhood to your very first memory. It may be hazy, but write out as much as you can recall. Jot down details. How old were you? Who is in the memory? Was it happy? Do you have pictures to help you remember?

APPLICATION

Go back to the ABC's and pick out exercises and questions that you wrote in three minutes. Now expand your writing. Write at least on page. Use the mountain top imagery for perspective and as a tool for writing large. Use humor or understanding. Feel free to choose a new word to write about. Before you begin, you may want to sit quietly, take a deep breath and imagine your river of life flowing. When you're ready, look down at each situation and see it fresh with new appreciation and generosity. Write large.

A. Anger. You wrote about a situation that made you very angry. Now go up to the mountaintop and use imagery as a tool for gaining perspective and writing with love and compassion. How can you see this situation from a different viewpoint? Where is the humor/Where is the larger view of humanity? Can you laugh at yourself for how this situation affected you?

B. Beliefs. Write about your beliefs about your body image when you were young. What character would you be in one of your favorite books or movies and why?

C. Childhood. Have a little chat with your sweet four-year-old self.

D. Decades. Choose one event from each decade and write about it with humor, gratitude, kindness, love, and acceptance. Write about defeat.

E. Excuse. Write about one excuse that keeps you from writing. Write about it as if you were a ten-year old. Write it as a humorous perspective.

F. Friend. Write about a falling out you had with a friend. Write about forbidden.

G. Gathering. Write about a family gathering. Write about guilt.

H. Humanity. Write about a character in your family from an amusing perspective

I. Ideals. Write about an issue that you felt passionate about when young. Has that changed? If you had a radio talk show, what would you rant about?

J. Joy. Just for today, look for joy around you, feel joyful, express joy. Write a page on joy. How has this expression of joy changed since you were a child?

K. Know. I know this much about divorce...I know this much about children...

L. Letters. Write a letter from your deathbed.

M. More. What do you want more of in your life? Write about metaphors and myths.

N. Nothing. Write about nothing but what is in front of you; the coffee cup, a pen.

O. Ordinary. What used to be ordinary, but now is extraordinary?

P. Perfect. Write about perfect. Write about proverbs. Write about parables.

Q. Quiet. Where does your heart go in stillness, in quiet times?

R. What I **remember** most about my childhood ___. What I can't remember ___.

S. Scrutinize a core event that was pivotal to the person you have become. What song would be your theme?

T. Themes. What themes or patterns emerged from this core event?

U. What quality has been **underutilized?** What would you like to nurture and grow?

V. Vast. Write about the vast wilderness of your heart. Write about vitality.

W. Wonder. How have you danced with wonder?

X. Using X-Ray vision, write about what you saw when you found the portal to the universe; heaven, cosmic realm, or a higher dimension.

Y. Yearn. Write about what you yearn for in your deepest heart.

Z. Zest. Tell me about your zest for living. Look at your river of life. It is full of twists and turns. Where does it zig? Where does it zag?

ANCESTORS

When I was doing research for my memoir, I found interesting stories about my ancestors. I remember a phrase I had come across that goes something like this: Suddenly all my ancestors are behind me. 'Be still' they say. 'Watch and listen. You are the result of the love of thousands. I felt that love. I marveled at their courage, hard work and sheer grit. Write about your ancestors. What do you know about your ancestors? What is most interesting? Gather pictures and stories and write about themes that become apparent. How did your grandparent's lives affect your parents? What values were passed down? What questions would you ask your great-grandparents if they were standing behind you?

Family Stories.

Facts: Write down how your family arrived to this country. List dates, people involved, places, etc. Gather pictures of your ancestors and obituaries.

Reflections: Do different people see family stories differently? For example, do various people in the family tell different stories about grandpa coming to America?

HIGHLIGHTS

Write 5 or 8 key points that tell the short story of your life.

Take any 10 years of your life and reduce them to 2 pages.

Think of a special trip you took or a place you loved to visit. What places made an impact on you?

What was one memorable character from your childhood?

Did you have a weird family member who didn't quite fit in?

What family member was truly kind?

Think of a challenging experience that was difficult for you to go through. How could this experience help others?

What was an awkward time for you in your life? When did you feel that you just didn't fit in? How did you overcome this feeling?

What was a seemingly trivial experience in your youth that you now know taught you an important lesson?

Who was a good storyteller when you were growing up?

What insight did you learn from these stories?

What fears did you have growing up? How did you overcome them?

Who is the person from your childhood you'd most like to spend more time with now?

BIRTH

Write about your birth. Can you recall any stories your parents told about your birth? How old were your parents? What were they like when you were born? What stories have you heard? What do the pictures reveal? What was going on in the larger world? Write about birth order. Describe where you lived. How did you get your name? Write about your earliest memory. Who cared for you as an infant and young child?

EARLY CHILDHOOD

What was the tone in your house? Look at pictures of yourself as a child. Choose one and focus on your posture, dress, facial expressions, and mood. What memories come up? Who was that child? What were you feeling? Who were your friends? Imagine a scene. How would you have walked, talked, what did you eat, and what games did you play? Who did you run to for comfort? Jot down the memories that come up.

Recall your early childhood religious experience. What mental picture did you have of God?

Mark a strong memory or turning point during later childhood (six-12) on your lifecycle. Describe this experience.

What happened to mark the end of your childhood? Tribal societies celebrated rites of passages and often involved prescribed steps in helping the child shift both inward and outward. Few rituals are in place in our society. When did you feel like an adult? Was there a turning point, event or situation where you felt independent? Mark it on your life cycle. What happened? How did it feel? When did you start to feel more independent?

Find a picture of you as a young child (five or under). Try to imagine this small you. Write about a scene from early childhood. What was going on around you? Were you a happy child? Think about the time, place and who would have been with you watching or taking the picture. What would they have been wearing? What was it like to be you as a young child? What sights, smells, sounds, tastes and textures do you remember? Recall an early experience or transition that you had as a young child such as the breakup of your parent's marriage, death of a grandparent, a move, changing schools, or losing a pet. How did you cope with change and transitions? Write or draw a picture of this experience. What do you remember about pre-school or the time before kindergarten? Did you have a traditional family? Speculate on what your mother and dad were wearing, thinking and feeling. What were you eating? Describe family meals and treats at special occasions. Consider these questions:

• Were you happy as a child?

• What games did you play? What was fun?

• Did you have pets? What was a typical day like in early childhood?

• What made your early childhood experience unique?

• What were the happiest times of your early childhood?

• If you could travel back and change one thing about your early childhood, what would it be?

The Event. What is one life event that happened in your early years that affected you or altered your life?

Love and Care. Who took care of you when you were 3 or 4? Who else was around you? Write about an early memory where you knew you were loved and felt cared for.

Do pleasant thoughts come to mind? Do you take a deep breath and marvel that you survived? What color would you paint your childhood? What was the tone in your house? Look at pictures of yourself as a child. Choose one and focus on your posture, dress, facial expressions, and mood. What memories come up? Who was that child? What were you feeling? Who were your friends? Imagine a scene. How would you have walked, talked, what did you eat, and what games did you play? Who did you run to for comfort? Jot down the memories that come up. Mark a strong memory or turning point during later childhood (six-12) on your lifecycle. Describe this experience.

What happened to mark the end of your childhood? Tribal societies celebrated rites of passages and often involved prescribed steps in helping the child shift both inward and outward. Few rituals are in place in our society. When did you feel like an adult? Was there a turning point, event or situation where you felt independent? Mark it on your life cycle. What happened? How did it feel?

Write about what you did after high school? Did you feel as if you had lots of choices?

LATER CHILDHOOD

Look at your lifecycle and mark a time around nine to twelve which you remember. What happened?

• Write about your siblings, playmates and your relationship with your parents during childhood.

• Create an image of a perfect evening? What were the sounds you remember? Draw or write about what you did.

• Where did you go to school? Were you teased? Did you have a favorite teacher? Who were your mentors? Who did you go for comfort? To whom did you tell your secrets? Describe a time you felt loved.

- Describe your favorites? What did you most enjoy about nature? What was most pleasing to you? What brought you joy?

- Did you go to church? Was this a positive experience? Do you still follow childhood teachings?

- Describe family rules. How were you disciplined? How were you rewarded, encouraged, and praised? How did you see yourself as a child? When did you feel confident and important?

- Describe achievements, vacations, how you celebrated holidays and birthdays. Describe how your family had fun. What were family rituals and customs? Describe typical meals. Where did you eat? Choose one birthday to write about.

- How would you rewrite your childhood?

- How did you feel that you were different from your family?

- Is there anyone you need to forgive from your childhood?

- Have you kept in touch with friends from your childhood?

- What major transitions did you or your family go through? How did it affect you?

- What music, books, TV shows and movies did you most enjoy? Did you perform in plays or musical events? Did you go to camp?

- Reminisce about a time when you were especially proud of an accomplishment or had an exciting adventure?

- What historical events were occurring during your childhood?

- Describe your mother's typical day. How do you remember her caring for you? Describe your dad's typical day. Describe a memory.

- What chores were you expected to do as a child? What lessons did you learn early on?

• What common childhood illnesses did you have? Did you have something more serious like polio? How did these frightening illnesses influence your family? Did your parents have home remedies? Were you ever in the hospital?

• What child influenced you most? What adult influenced you most? How did your parents handle money? Did your parents talk about money to your?

• Was there an event in your childhood that was difficult? Describe a painful memory that changed you. Did your parents talk to you about your confusion or pain? What got you through it?

• What death do you remember as a child and how did it affect you?

• When you think of the tone of your childhood, what comes to mind? What smells, sights, sounds, books, and songs do you associate with childhood?

• Describe fears. How did you deal with them? Who protected you? When were you homesick?

• How were you let down or hurt?

• What did you take for granted? To whom would you like to say, "Thank You?"

• If you could time travel back and change one thing about your childhood, what would it be?

THE END OF CHILDHOOD

Tribal societies celebrated rites of passages and often involved prescribed steps in helping the child shift both inward and outward. Few rituals are in place in our society. When did you feel like an adult? Was there a turning point, event or situation where you felt independent? Mark it on your life cycle. What happened? How did it feel?
Write about what you did after high school? Did you feel as if you had lots of choices?

Write about an event or turning point that marked the end of childhood. Write about your experience and how it was different from your siblings, parents and grandparents. Consider:

• Did you have a rite of passage, ritual or celebration that marked leaving childhood? How did you test the waters? Did you venture out and then come back?

• Do you think you grew up too fast? Was there an experience that was difficult during this time?

• Did you have a positive self-image about yourself?

• Was the transition to middle school difficult? Who were your friends? Were you worried about fitting in? Did you like school? Did you find you were well prepared for high school?

• What were your parents like during this period of childhood? Did you feel close? Did you talk often? Were they supportive? How did they discipline you?

• Did you experience drinking or drugs during this time?

• Describe a scene having to do with beginning to date or hang out with classmates.

• Write about a vacation or trip you took when you were 12 or 13.

• If you could time travel back, what would you change?

• What advice do you have for a child of 11 or 12 who wishes they were grown up and had more freedom.

ADOLESCENCE

Mark the start of adolescence on your lifecycle. Find a picture of you as a teenager. What were your general feelings? What color would best illustrate your mood? Do a mind map with as many memories as you can recall. Then reflect and write about this period.

Adolescence is often an awkward, challenging and sometimes painful transition that marks the central issue of shifting from dependency to independence. Bodies are changing, emotions are running wild, and the issues of relationships and belonging become paramount. The carefree days of childhood are over and big questions in life are addressed such as "Who am I?" "How can I fit in?" "Where will I go to college or what kind of job will I get?" "What are my beliefs and convictions?" "What is meaningful to me?" Psychologist, Eric Erickson wrote that adolescents must achieve a sense of identity in terms of values and self-esteem as well as resolve the role confusion around work, sex roles, politics, and religion. How did you struggle with these issues? Who made it easier for you? How was it difficult?

Did you want to be more independent? What freedoms did your parents give you? Did you make a fashion statement? Describe an outfit you wore that made an impression.

HIGH SCHOOL

Remember, you survived high school. Now you can tell your story.

REFLECT ON THESE QUESTIONS:

Describe your high school and your most vivid memories. What were your favorite classes and activities? Who were your friends? Do you still stay in contact? As you write, imagine sights, smells, sounds, tastes, textures, songs, dances, clothes, and styles.

• How did you feel about yourself as a teenager? Was your self-image positive? Were you confident? What did you do well? What were your talents, favorite subjects, sports? Were you involved in church and community?

• What dreams did you have? What opportunities did you let go by? Did you earn your own spending money?

• Describe your first crush. Describe a romance that broke your heart. Did you break someone's heart? Describe dates, prom and parties. What made a fun evening? When did you feel accepted?

M is for Memoir

- What were family rules? How were you talked to about drugs, alcohol, sex, smoking and dating? When did your family begin to treat you as an adult? Describe your relationship with your parents and siblings. How did they handle conflict?

- How was adolescence different from your parents and grandparents?

- When did you learn to drive? Were you a safe driver?

- Describe a time that was painful or confusing?

- When were you worried or fearful? How did you get through tough times?

- Describe a wonderful memory or an exciting experience.

- Who encouraged you to excel? Did your education prepare you for college or the world of work?

- What did you wish your parents could have given you in terms of support or encouragement?

- What did you appreciate about your parents?

- Did you have to shoulder adult responsibilities or feel as if you grew up too fast?

- What important values did you learn as a teenager?

- Did you have a problem saying "no" to peer pressure? How did you develop a sense of identity and self-esteem?

- Write about what you did after high school? Did you feel as if you had lots of choices?

- What did you take for granted? Who would you say "thank you" to today?

- If you could take a time machine back to high school, what would you do differently?

- Write about graduating from high school, how you celebrated and the excitement. If you didn't graduation, describe the circumstances. Did you get your GED? Do you regret dropping out?

- What advice would you give to a teenager today?

Exercise: Draw a picture, sketch a scene or create a sand tray to symbolically illustrate a time in your youth that was painful or brought you shame and that you have trouble writing or talking about to others. How can you integrate this experience into the whole? What understanding about you and others involved could help heal?

> The silence of the spheres is the music of a wedding feast. The more we persist in misunderstanding the phenomena of life, the more we analyze them out into strange finalities and complex purposes of our own, the more we involve ourselves in sadness. But it does not matter much because no despair of ours can alter the reality of things, or stain the joy of the cosmic dance which is always there.
>
> -*Thomas Merton*

EARLY ADULTHOOD

Like the end of childhood, becoming an adult is for some people a gradual process and for others it is abrupt. Mark your life cycle of early adulthood. When did you take on more adult responsibilities and tackle the big questions: Who am I? What is my purpose? What will become of me? Describe a scene from early adulthood.

What was the most memorable experience of this time? Consider the following:

- Did you decide to go to college or not? What were the issues? What helped you decide? Did you know what you wanted to major in or the career you hoped to enter?

- If you went into the military, describe that experience.

- If you went to college, how did you adjust? Did you live away from home? What are your key memories about college? Did you work part-time?

• If you went to work fulltime, what did you do? Where did you live? Write about your first jobs. If you went to the military, write about this experience and what you learned.

• Describe major transitions that you went through in your 20's.

• Describe your relationships in your 20's. Do you still stay in touch with friends? Did you date a lot?

• What helped you define your identity?

• What opportunities were given to you? What opportunities did you create?

• Who would you most like to thank for helping you through these years?

• Describe your highs and lows during this time.

• What did you learn the "hard way?"

• Write about your relationships during this stage. Did you have several serious relationships? Did you ever feel used or that you were using people? What did you learn?

• Write about graduating from college and coping with finding a job, creating a career, living on your own and making your way in the world.

• Describe the places you lived in your 20's. Do you still have friends from that time? Write about a really fun event, a deep and meaningful relationship or a moving experience.

• Did you follow rules or did you get in trouble on campus or in the community with alcohol or other drugs?

• Did you have more serious problems with the law? Did you spend time in jail or prison? Write about your experiences. What was the turning point? What choices led you to spiral downward? How did your experiences in childhood and adolescent lead to getting into trouble?

• What did you take for granted? Who would you say, "thank you" to?

• If you could time travel back, what would you change?

• What advice would you give to a young adult?

• How did you adjust to freedom, handle finances, do laundry, make new friends, get along with a roommate, schedule time, cope with pressures, and meet deadlines?

LATER ADULTHOOD

Mark the turning point on your life cycle that signals a settling down phase of adulthood. Draw a picture of one item or experience of an item, possession or event that clearly marked a time of responsibility and the end of youth. What was the most memorable experience of this time? Consider:

• If you married during this time, describe how your life changed.

• If you had children during this time, describe the impact they had on your life.

• What was it like to juggle school, work and family responsibilities?

• Describe your later 20's, where you lived, your friends and experiences. Describe your early 30's and how life changed as you left your 20's. Who were your friends? Do you still have friends from your late 20's and early 30's? Did you follow your dreams?

Mark the start of your career on your life cycle. Draw a picture of your first real job on your career path. Write about how you chose this career and the joys and challenges. What was your most memorable experience? Include pictures or drawings of you at particularly high and low periods. Consider:

• Write about job changes and early challenges in your career. Were you fired, demoted or laid off? Describe that experience. Describe your worst and best boss.

• Write about career disappointments, problems with co-workers and setbacks. How did you deal with the daily grind of working can provide major life lessons?

• Describe promotions and career highs.

• Is this the career you dreamed about? Did your career fit your talents, values, personality and needs?

• Did you take career risks? Did you follow your dreams?

• If you could time travel back, what would you change in your career?

• What career advice would you give someone starting?

• How did your career change over time?

• How did you choose your career direction? Describe your first real job.

• Did you have difficulty choosing a college major or a career path?

• Did you intentionally plan and choose a career or did you drift into a job?

Consider these questions:
• If you decided not to have children, when did you make this decision and why? Write about the circumstances, the time, the issues and whether it was a difficult decision. Do you feel as if you missed something or is your life fulfilled? How has this decision changed your life? Write about the children in your life. Who do you want to pass on life lessons and values?

- Write about your decision to have children. Did you made a conscious decision to have children or did you drift into it or was it a surprise? Were you looking forward to having children?

- Did you have children young? Were you ready for this commitment? What surprised you most about having children?

- In what ways are you like your parents and what ways did you decide to raise children differently?

- Did you enjoy your children?

- If you could time travel back, what would you do differently?

FAMILIES

Tell me about your family.

Families today are different than families a hundred years ago. People move, extended families living close are rare, and people have more choices about having children and how they define family.

- As a child or young adult, what was your image of a perfect family?

- What kind of family did you want to create?

- Did you want a loving partner only, one child, two kids, or a number of kids?

- How is your family different than your parent's family or your earlier idealized version of family?

- List the people in your life who you consider to be part of your family.

PARENTS

If you are like most people, you may find it hard to write about your parents. Look at the big issues: love, sacrifice, devotion, resentment, breaking away, control, abuse, or abandonment. These memories return again and again. Coming to terms with childhood memories, painful events and memories can be a struggle. It is worth the time and effort.

MOTHER AND FATHER

Facts: On one page, write all the facts you know about your mother and father: full name, occupation, nationality, religion, education, birth, date of birth, siblings and the names of their parents. If you were raised by a single parent, were orphaned, adopted, raised by aunts, uncles, or grandparents, never knew a parent, had a parent in prison, step-parents, foster parents or a parent left you early in life, explain the facts and how you felt, coped and how you see it now.

RELATIVES

Tell a story about a relative that you just didn't know and seemed a mystery. Tell a story of a relative who had secrets that were whispered. Tell a story about a relative who lied or stretched the truth. Who was the most unusual relative in your family?

HERO

Was there a major figure in your life that made an impact on you? Who was your hero growing up and why? Who was a real-life villain? What story stays with you even now?

Reflection: Jot down memories, stories, events, and traits and characteristics. Describe physical characteristics. What did you call your parents? Were they warm, loving, supportive and kind or cool, distant, harsh? Was it a combination of the two? Were they very involved and demonstrative? Do you remember them playing with you, reading to you, taking you on trips or to lunch alone? Did they have a sense of humor? List one word that best describes each of your parents. Find a photo that captures their essence. Consider the following:

- What were their talents and gifts?

- What were their hopes and dreams?

- Do you think they realized their dreams?

- How would your parent's life have been different if born in a different time and place?

- If you could time travel back, what is one day or event you'd change regarding your parents?

- What is your earliest memory you have of your parents?

- Write about the humorous events with each of your parents.

- Describe some of your best and happiest times together.

Write about other issues you may have experienced such as divorce, stepparents, foster parents, adoptive parents, homelessness, moving often, etc.

CHILDREN

Write about children.

- Describe the birth of your children. Your age, place, dates, etc.

- Reflect on how having children changed your life. What were you unprepared for in being a parent?

- Describe one early memory when you felt absolute love for your child.

- Describe a time when you felt confused, exhausted or overwhelmed. How did you bounce back?

- Describe one memorable family vacation.

- What simple, everyday activities did you most enjoy?

- What rules did you have as a parent?

- Did you and your spouse have similar views about discipline? What were the differences?

- What did you do right?

- What would you do differently?

- If you could time travel back, what day or event would you change?

- What advice do you have for new parents?

- Do you have forgiveness issues around being a parent?

- If you chose not to have children, write about this decision. What are positive factors? Do you have any regrets?

- Write a short letter to each of your children

- If you were unable to have children, write about how this affected your life. If you miscarried or had an abortion, write about these losses and how they shaped your life.

EARLY MID-LIFE

Look on your life cycle and pinpoint the time you considered to be early mid-life. Write about the most memorable experience of this time.

Carl Jung said, "After 40, every question is a spiritual question... The worst of it all is that intelligent and cultivated people live their lives without even knowing of the possibility of such transformations. Wholly unprepared, they embark upon the second half of life. We cannot live the afternoon of life according to the program of life's morning; for what was great in the morning will be little at evening, and what in the morning was true will at evening become a lie."

Consider these questions:
- What was your life like in your 40's and early 50's?

- Did you feel "middle aged?"

- Was mid-life a period of calm and fulfillment?

- Did you settled into the career you wanted or did you change careers?

- Did you build strong relationships?

- Did you have a better sense of yourself and what is important in life?

- Describe a time of inward upheaval and transformation?

- Did you go through a classic "mid-life crisis?"

- Did you have regrets for what you had not accomplished?

- Did you grieve over the loss of your youth?

- What caused you to come to grips with reality? Did you use the word "never" in conversation e.g., "I'm never going to have children," "I'm never going to meet my soul mate," or "I'm never going to become a famous artist or CEO of the company."

- How did your parents cope with mid-life?

- Did you go through a time of reassessing values and beliefs?

- How would you describe your spiritual life? Is your religious faith different than how you were raised? Is your spiritual life stronger than when you were younger?

- How have you coped with growing older?

- What major transition did you have to cope with during this time?

- If you could time travel back what would you do differently?

- If you were giving advice to someone going through mid-life, what would you say?

> My fiftieth year had come and gone,
> I sat, a solitary man,
> In a crowded London shop,
> An open book and empty cup
> On the marble table-top.
> While on the shop and street I gazed
> My body of a sudden blazed;
> And twenty minutes more or less
> It seemed, so great my happiness,
> That I was blessed and could bless."
>
> -W. B. Yeats

LATER MID-LIFE

Look on your life cycle and pinpoint a few memories that pop up that reflect this period. Write about the most memorable experience of this time.

People are living longer, more active lives and people in their later 50's and 60's can still be vital and youthful. Many people have told me that this was the phase when they felt stability and renewal since their health was still good, they had more money to do what they wanted to do, their children were raised and on their own and their careers were winding down or they had just retired or started a new career.

Consider these questions:
• Did you have your finances in order and feel comfortable about retirement?

• How is your relationship with your grown children?

• What were your parents like in their 50's and 60's?

• How has your relationship changed with your spouse?

• If you retired, did you have enough interests to stay active, involved and busy?

• How did you cope with the loss of family and friends?

• What was the major transition that you coped with during this time?

• If you've retired, describe what it felt like to make this transition. Describe your career. How long did you work? Was it a traditional 9-5, was it high-pressured, did you like your work or were you ready for a change? How long have you been retired?

• How did you spend your days when you first retired?

• What did you miss most about your job?

• How did you find a sense of purpose and direction?

• How did your relationship with your spouse change?

• How did your relationship with friends and family change? What have you always wanted to do once your retired that you did?

• What have you always wanted to do that you haven't done yet?

• What surprised you about retirement?

• What transition did you go through at this time?

• If you could time travel back, what change would you make in planning for your retirement?

• What advice would you give to others?

RELATIONSHIPS

> "Each relationship you have with another person reflects the relationship you have with yourself."
>
> -Alice Deville

Friendships. Write about a friendship that has sustained you during a rough time. Go back over what you have written about friendships. Who were your closest friends? Who are your closest friends? Are you still in touch with childhood, high school, college friends?

First Love. Describe your first love. Did you marry this person? If not, would your life have been different if you had? If you broke up, what happened? How did you feel? How did you bounce back? Include facts such as dates, ages, names, places, and events. How did you feel at the time? Write about how you felt at the time and how you feel now with reflection and perspective.

Siblings. Write about each of your siblings listing all the facts you can find. Reflect on your relationship with each one. If you're estranged or have a difficult relationship, what happened? What could you do that might help heal this relationship?

Write about your siblings now. If you were an only child, write about that experience.

MARRIAGE

Marriage has changed in the last 40 years. It is now optional, more broadly defined, and people marry later. Even thought the statistics emphasize that marriage is a risky business, most people long for a deep, intimate relationship.

• Describe the proposal. Draw or include a picture of your wedding or commitment ceremony. Describe the setting, place, food, music, color and honeymoon.

• Did you feel that you knew each other well? What did you have in common? How were you different? What surprised you most about your partner?

• What was the initial attraction? Why did you fall in love with this person? What qualities and values do you value most? How were you alike and different?

• Describe how long you dated, a typical date, and an event that stands out that helped you make the decision to marry.

• Did you feel as though you made a conscious decision or did you drift into marriage?

- Were family and friends supportive?

- Did you have doubts? Were you both committed to the same goals and values? What is one quality about your partner that you didn't know until after your were married?

- What surprised you most about marriage?

- How did you handle disagreements or problems?

- What adjustments did you make to make your marriage better?

- What kept your marriage together? What would have made it happier?

- Describe a time when you were fully present for your partner.

- What were your biggest challenges? Did you have a crisis to get through? What adjustments did you have to make?

- Recall your greatest joys and some of the happiest times of your marriage.

- What are the qualities you are most thankful for in your spouse?

- What do you wish you had done differently in your early marriage?

- Draw or describe your first house. What was a typical day like in your first year? Who were your friends?

- If you could time travel back, what would you change about your marriage?

- Do you have any forgiveness issues surrounding your marriage?

- What have you learned through this relationship?

DIVORCE OR BREAKUP

Write about divorce. How has it affected you or those you know?

If you divorced or had a breakup of a long relationship, describe the experience. Was it painful, difficult, confusing or liberating or both?

• What circumstances, reasons, feelings and turning points led to the split? Describe how you felt when you first decided or were told that the marriage was over.

• When did you learn that your marriage was over? Was there a defining moment or years of friction?

• How did you handle the breakup? What were your thoughts and feelings? How did you deal with your anger or your partner's anger?

• Describe your emotions? What were your greatest fears?

• What feelings surprised you most?

• To whom did you go for help? Who supported you?

• What was the best advice you heard?

• What helped you most to get through this difficult time?

• What did you miss most about being married?

• What about the breakup was healthy and what was unhealthy? What did you do to make the breakup easier?

• If you had children, what did you do to create harmony and focus on their needs?

• How did your partner's qualities lead to the breakup?

• What qualities kept you from being a better partner?

- Did you blame your partner exclusively or did you face your part in the breakup?

- How have you changed since the divorce? What did you learn from the experience?

- If you could time travel back, what would you change?

- What message would give your ex today?

- What advice would you give someone thinking about or going through a divorce?

- Do you have forgiveness issues around your divorce?

Remarriage or New Companionship. Write about marrying again. Many people who have lost their partner through death or divorce, can't see themselves marrying again. What a pleasant surprise when they fall in love again. My mother was 87 when she remarried years after my dad had died. She found companionship and laughter after years of loneliness. If you remarried, describe the experience.

- Describe what it was like to find love again.

- How did friends and family react?

- Did you feel guilty or that you were betraying your first marriage or children?

- When did you feel certain that this was a good choice?

- What attracted you? How is this new relationship different?

- What did you learn about creating healthy relationships?

- What transition did you experience when dating again or meeting new people?

- If you could time travel back, what changes would you make?

- What advice would you give someone who has found love again and is thinking about marrying?

- What did you learn through this relationship?

AGING

If you have experienced this time of life, write about it. If not, write from the perspective of what you want your old age to look like. Will you be a wise sage? Will you have lessons to pass on? What do you want this time of your life to look like?

Early Old Age. There's a saying, "You're not old until you're 90. Before that age, you are in early old age or just aging. Many people in their 60's and 70's are active, working, helping young adult children and generally feeling good, just older. If you've reached the age of 60 or beyond, write about what it feels like to begin the process of aging. What is changing in your body and mind? What surprised you about growing older? Do you feel a richness about life? What has been the most difficult experience? What has been the most rewarding? Is your life fuller? How are you preparing for later old age? Consider the transitions that occurred in your early old age and write a few sentences. Write about your 60's. Write about your 70's.

Retirement. If you retired, how did you handle it? What fills up your life? Did you go back to work, start a business or work part-time? After retirement, did you have time to spend with special friends and family? Did you feel that there is a lack of urgency and frantic achievement that dominates earlier stages of life? Some people say that this can be a time of quiet reflection, active involvement in personal interests and community projects. Tell me about how you handled retirement and early old age.

Later Old Age. If you're lucky enough to live to 80, 90 and beyond, how have you adjusted to old age? What was the hardest transition? Did you give up driving, living alone? Tell me about loss. If you lived into your 90's, loss is inevitable. There is the loss of many good friends, often a spouse and sometimes even a child. The body doesn't bounce back from illness, more joints and muscles hurt, there is a general loss of mobility, energy, and diminished sight and hearing. If you're younger, how would you like to be as an elder? What will you look like? How will you spend your days? Where will you live? Who will be around you? Visualize this stage and write about your hopes and wishes.

- Who do you know who has aged well? What lessons did you learn?

- How are you planning for old age?

- How did your parents handle aging?

- How do you feel about getting older?

- What do you consider old?

- How have your values changed?

- Are you more tolerant of people?

- Describe your relationship with your children.

- What have you learned most about life?

- What do you have faith in? How do you express your spiritual life?

- How do you feel about life right now? What are you looking forward to?

- What is the biggest transition you've gone through at this time?

- What are you most grateful for?

- If you could give advice to someone who is going through the aging process, what would it be?

If You Could Live Your Life Again. If you had it to do all over again, what would you do differently?

If I Had My Life to Live Again

"If I had my life to live over again, I'd dare to make more mistakes next time. I'd relax. I'd limber up. I'd be sillier than I've been this trip. I would take fewer things seriously. I would take more chances, I would take more trips, I would climb more mountains and swim more rivers. I would eat more ice cream and less beans. I would, perhaps, have more actual troubles but fewer imaginary ones. You see, I'm one of those people who was sensible and sane, hour after hour, day after day. Oh, I've had my moments. If I had it to do over again, I'd have more of them. In fact, I'd try to have nothing else—just moments, one after another, instead of living so many years ahead of each day. I've been one of those persons who never goes anywhere without a thermometer, a hot-water bottle, a raincoat, and a parachute. If I could do it again, I would travel lighter than I have. If I had my life to live over, I would start barefoot earlier in the spring and stay that way later in the fall. I would go to more dances, I would ride more merry-go-rounds, I would pick more daisies."

-Nadine Stair

DEATH

Death has been referred to as the great teacher. Facing mortality can prompt you to examine and understand your life, what it meant and what lessons you can pass on. Through reflection and writing you can discover the deeper meaning of your life, what you have meant to others, what you stand for. By examining your spiritual beliefs, death may be the most integrating of all our life's experiences and lead us to wholeness. A life review can be healing, illuminate the shadows, fill up the empty spaces. Isn't that what we all want, to die in the fullness of being? How can we prepare for losing the people we love most? How can we prepare for our own death? One way is by doing what you've been doing—the life review. Reflecting, remembering, writing and sharing helps make sense out of your life. Another way to prepare for death is by getting to the essence of what matters most. If you still have your parents, talk with them, ask them questions and give them the three most important messages. Think of what you would say if you could go back and talk with a parent who has died. By talking, writing and sharing stories we can heal our relationships.

> "The living self has one purpose only: to come into its own fullness of being; as a tree comes into full blossom or a bird into spring beauty."
>
> -D.H. Lawrence,

Your First Experience of Death. Write about your earliest experience of death. Who died? What happened? How did it affect you? Write about your most profound experience of death. What happened? Write about a time when you experienced real grief.

Death of Parents

How old were your parents when they died? How did you cope with this loss? What gifts and sayings live on through you?

> "No one eve told me that grief felt so like fear. I am not afraid, but the sensation is like being afraid The same fluttering in the stomach, the same restlessness, the yawning. I keep on swallowing…"
>
> -C.S. Lewis

The Death of a Child. If you lost a child, write about this profound experience. Who do you know that lost a child? Write about how that experience affected you.

> "Where you used to be, there is a hole in the world, which I find myself constantly walking around in the daytime, and falling into at night."
>
> -Edna St. Vincent Millay

Death of a Partner. If you have lost a spouse or partner write about this experience.
Describe the events, time, place, your age, how long you had been together and circumstances. Draw or describe the scene when you first found out the news. What were your first thoughts and feelings? What do you remember most? How did your body react? What was the first week like and how did you get through it?

- What motions did you go through immediately after the death? What feelings surprised you? What were your fears?

• What rituals or ceremony helped you most? Described your best support. Did you get unexpected support from someone?

• Who was there to help and support you? Was this a surprise?

• What could they have done differently?

• Write about your friends and how they helped.

• What comforted you? What made your pain more bearable?

• What could you have used at the time? Did someone do too much? What resources did you most appreciate?

• What mistake did you make at this time?

• What was the biggest surprised you faced living alone?

• What feelings took you by surprised? Did you do something "crazy" that you couldn't believe?

• Does anyone understand your grief?

• Describe how your life changed? What surprised you the most about being on your own? What did you miss most when the initial shock wore off and your life returned to "normal?"

• What were the turning points of your recovering and healing?

• How did you cope with your grief? What activities helped you get through this through this time of intense grief? Did people expect something from you that you were unable to give?

• Describe your loneliness. What did you do that helped?

• What decisions seemed overwhelming?

• Describe the turning points when your grief changed and you took a step forward.

- How did your friendships change? Your entertaining and social life?

- How have you changed? What did you discover about yourself?

- What issues of forgiveness did you face and resolve?

- If you could time travel back, what would you do differently?

- What advice would you give someone who is coping with the loss of a partner?

Your Death. In a sense, all of life's transitions are preparing for the great transition of dying. If you are fortunate, you leave a legacy of love and a memoir of your life story. What is your goal? For me, it is to love and live an authentic life and die in the fullness of being surrounded by loved ones; that would be quite enough. What do you want your last few years to be like on this earth? Where do you want to live? Where do you want to die? What gifts to you hope to pass on? If you had a choice, what kind of death would you like? (Sudden, dignified, slow enough to plan, doing what you love, etc.) What is one thing you'd like to complete before you die?

Carl Jung said that the task of each of us in this lifetime is to follow the path of individuation... *"a way of attaining liberation by one's own efforts and finding the courage to be oneself."* But, who are we? What do we want? What truly matters? There is a story about an old, wise rabbi, named Azusa who said, *"When I was a young man, I feared that when I died, God was going to ask me why I was not more like Moses. Now that I am an old man, I fear that when I die God will ask me why I wasn't more like Azusa."* I believe that our children want us to be who we really are in the fullness of our being. Go back to the Three Big Questions and reflect on what you wrote. Add to your answer.

Write your obituary. Really. What do you want to be said about you in the paper?

Plan your memorial. What would you like? Where will the service be held? Who will conduct the service? What music will be played? What tone do you want it to convey?

Write your eulogy. What would you like others to say about you?

Looking Ahead and Within

> "What lies behind us and what lies before us are tiny matters compared to what lies within us."
>
> *-Oliver Wendell Holmes*

> "If you stand right front and face to face with a fact, you will see the sun glimmer on both its surfaces as if it were a scimitar, and you will feel its sweet edge dividing you thorough your heart and marrow. Be it life or death, we crave only reality."
>
> *-Henry David Thoreau*

As you look ahead and within, reflect on the **Three Big Questions** presented at the start of the book. Record specific facts, dates and people and also a reflection of how you feel about your beliefs then and now with perspective. List specific beliefs such as hard work, family, honesty, religion, and relationships.

Who am I? Go back to the introduction and the exercise, 'Who Am I. 'Add to your memory cluster now that you've gone through many of these exercises.

Reflect. Write about being real and authentic. What beliefs and principles guide you? Have you challenge old beliefs that no longer work for you? Have you questioned and really examined where these beliefs come from and if they are based on reason? When did you acquire your beliefs, from whom, what was the event or circumstances? What gives you the most joy about your beliefs? How do they limit you? Were they formed through organized religion? What do you want out of life?

The great philosopher, Alan Watts once remarked that the most revolutionary question that any of us can ask is, "What do I want?"

Fear. What are three things you fear? Is death one of them? How do you feel about the last big transition? Is death a door to a new beginning or just the end? What are your spiritual beliefs about death? How are you preparing for your death?

The Shadows. To become friends with the shadows and allow them to merge with the light is to grow up. No one really wants to grow up and take responsibility but it is the only way to be authentic. No one ever expects perfection. Realness will do nicely. You don't have to beat the shadows or hate the darkness or make excuses, justify or blame. You don't have to make dramatic confessions or hurt people with your rationalization of unloading. Just turn on the light and the darkness is over. See beyond the shadows and whenever possible quietly making amends, asking and extending forgiveness. Have you confronted your shadows?

What shadow have you kept hidden? What would happen if you let your mask fall and revealed your true self? What would happen if you embraced the whole of your being—all your faults and shortcomings?

> "I went to the woods because I wished to live deliberately, to front only the essential facts of life, and see if I could not learn what it had to teach and not, when I came to die, discover that I had not lived."
>
> *-Henry David Thoreau*

Why am I here? What is My Purpose? Go back to the Introduction and the exercise, 'Why am I Here?' Add to your memory cluster.

Reflect. Write about what is essential? What lessons do you want to pass on? What advice do you have to give help the next generation? What is your legacy? What matters most?

What will Become of Me? How to be with death and dying. Go back to the Introduction and the exercise, 'What will Become of Me?' Add to your memory cluster?

Reflect. Write about what you still want to do to fulfill your life? What goals do you still want to accomplish? If you're lucky enough to live to a ripe old age, what kind of person do you want to be? Visualize a wise old sage in good health, happy and content. Where do you live? Who is around you? Do you have fulfilling relationships and a full life? Do you want to keep learning and growing?

What is to become of your story? Will you make writing your memoir a priority?

Death
What will you miss when you die?

Reflect on this quote from **Rumi:**

> "I placed one foot on the wide plane of death, and some grand immensity sounded on the emptiness. I have felt nothing ever like the wild wonder of that moment."

> "Catastrophes are the essence of the spiritual path, the series of breakdowns allowing us to discover the threads that weave all of life into a whole cloth."
> *-Roshi*

LESSONS

You could focus your writing around lessons that you learned and want to pass on. What advice do you want to give? Think of your audience. Who will read your memoir? Think of someone picking up your memoir a hundred years from now. Write as if you are able to time travel back and talk to a few of your future ancestors. Read your work aloud. Think of talking with them around a campfire. There they are; your cherished great grandchildren or great, great nieces listening to every word. Keep it simple. Remember three points:

1. Tell them what happened. What did you notice? What did you desire, need or want?

2. Tell them how you felt. What thoughts and feelings were going on within you? Describe the struggle.

3. Tell them what you learned. What were the lessons you want to pass on? What is your best advice?

What Matters: Your LEGACY:
What values would you most want to hand down to your children, grandchildren and great grandchildren or future generations?

- What have you fought for in life and that you think is worth fighting for?

- Who taught you the most during your lifetime?

- Who are or were your heroes?

- What was your greatest challenge in life?

- Describe a transition or experience that you will never forget.

- What have you been fully committed to in your life?

- What is your life view?

- Is life a struggle or is life courting you, embracing and delighting you and inviting you deeper into joy?

- What have you learned that has helped you most in life?

- What practical coping skills would you like to hand down to future generations?

- What act of forgiveness has meant the most to you?

- What would you tell your children about forgiveness?

- What spiritual values do you want to hand down?

- What have you learned about loving others?

- What have you learned about coping with pain and loss?

Letters to Children, Grandchildren, Future Generations

Humorist Sam Levinson wrote in a letter, *"...to my grandchildren and children everywhere. Leaving you everything I have had in my lifetime: a good family, respect for learning, compassion for my fellowman, and some four-letter words for all occasions like help, give, care, feel and love."*

M is for Memoir

Write the life lessons you want to pass on:

Sharon K. Ferrett

Reflect on the following and write a few lines about how they relate to you:

"Someday, after we have mastered the winds, the waves, the tide and gravity, we shall harness for God the energies of love. Then, for the second time in the history of the world, man will have discovered fire."
-Teilhard De Chardin

"The silence of the spheres is the music of a wedding feast. The more we persist in misunderstanding the phenomena of life, the more we analyze them out into strange finalities and complex purposes of our own, the more we involve ourselves in sadness. But it does not matter much because no despair of ours can alter the reality of things, or stain the joy of the cosmic dance which is always there."
-Thomas Merton

As Joseph Campbell said, "There is a track just waiting there for each of us, and once on it, doors will open that were not open before and would not open for anyone else. Everything does start clicking along and, yes, even Mother Nature herself supports the journey. I have found that you do have only to take that one step toward the gods and they will then take ten steps toward you."

Maj. Sullivan Ballou's July 1861 message to his wife, Sarah, written a week before he died at the Battle of Bull Run:
"The memories of the blissful moments I have spent with you come creeping over me, and I feel most gratified to God and to you that I have enjoyed them so long," he wrote. "And hard it is for me to give them up and burn to ashes the hopes of future years, when God willing, we might still have lived and loved together, and seen our sons grow up to honorable manhood around us. Never forget how much I love you, and when my last breath escapes me on the battlefield, it will whisper your name."
-Column for April 12

"I went to the woods because I wished to live deliberately, to front only the essential facts of life, and see if I could not learn what it had to teach and not, when I came to die, discover that I had not lived."
-Henry David Thoreau

"Birdsong rings relief to my longing.
I am just as ecstatic as they are,
But with nothing to say;
Please, universal soul, practice some song, or something through me."
-Rumi

Though face and form alter with the years,
I hold fast to the pearl of my mind.
-Han-Shan

And Now We Will Count to Twelve
and we will all keep still.
For once on the face of the earth
let's not speak in any language;
let's stop for one second,
and not move our arms so much.
It would be an exotic moment
without rush, without engines,
we would all be together
in a sudden strangeness.
Fishermen in the cold sea
would not harm whales
and the man gathering salt
would look at his hurt hands.
Those who prepare green wars,
wars with gas, wars with fire,
victory with no survivors,
would put on clean clothes
and walk about with their brothers
in the shade doing nothing.
What I want should not be confused
with total inactivity.

(Life is what it is about;
I want no truck with death.)
If we were not so single-minded
about keeping our lives moving,
and for once could do nothing,
perhaps a huge silence
might interrupt this sadness
of never understanding ourselves
and of threatening ourselves with death.
Perhaps the earth can teach us
as when everything seems dead
and later proves to be alive.
Now I'll count up to twelve,
and you keep quiet and I will go.
                              -*Pablo Neruda*

"When I was a boy and I would see scary things in the news, my mother would say to me, 'Look for the helpers.' You will always find people who are helping!"
                              -*Fred Rogers*

OLD AGE

Write about what you think you'll be like as an old person. Consider this poem:

Otherwise
I got out of bed
On two strong legs.
It might have been
Otherwise. I ate
Cereal, sweet
Milk, ripe, flawless
Peach. It might
Have been otherwise.
I took the dog uphill
To the birch wood.
All morning I did
The work I love.

M is for Memoir

At noon, I lay down
With my mate. It might
Have been otherwise.
We ate dinner together
At a table with silver
Candlesticks. It might
Have been otherwise.
I slept in a bed
In a room with paintings
On the walls, and
Planned another day
Just like this day.
But one day, I know,
It will be otherwise.

-Jane Kenyon

Collect poems and stories that speak to you. Here are a few of my favorites:

"One day the sun admitted,
I'm just a shadow.
I wish I could show you
The Infinite incandescence
That has cast my brilliant image!
I wish I could show you,
when you are lonely or in darkness,
the astonishing light of your own being."

-Rumi

The Journey
By Mary Oliver

One day you finally knew what you had to do,
and began though the voices around you kept shouting
their bad advice.
Though the whole house began to tremble
and you felt the old tug at your ankles.
"Mend my life?" Each voice cried.
But you didn't stop.

You knew what you had to do, though the wind pried with its stiff
fingers at the very foundation,
though their melancholy was terrible.
It was already late enough and a wild night,
And the road full of fallen branches and stones.
But little by little, as you left their voices behind,
The stars began to burn through the sheets of clouds,
And there was a new voice which you slowly recognize as your own
that kept you company as you strode deeper and deeper into the world
determined to do the only thing you could do—determined
to save the only life you could save.

To Bless the Space Between Us
by John O'Donohue.

"May you be blessed by the holy names of those
Who, without you knowing it,
Help to carry and lighten your pain.
May you know serenity
When you are called
To enter the house of suffering.
May a window of light always surprise you.
May you be granted the wisdom
To avoid false resistance
When suffering knocks on the door of your life,
May you glimpse the eventual gifts.

May memory bless and protect you
With the hard-earned light of past travail;
To remind you that you have survived before
And though the darkness now is deep
You will soon see approaching light.

May you know that though the storm might rage,
Not a hair of your head will be harmed.

M is for Memoir

The following was written by Regina Brett, 90 years old, of The Plain Dealer, Cleveland, Ohio

" To celebrate growing older, I once wrote the 45 lessons life taught me. It is the most-requested column I've ever written. My odometer rolled over to 90 in August, so here is the column once more:" 1. Life isn't fair, but it's still good. 2. When in doubt, just take the next small step. 3. Life is too short to waste time hating anyone. 4. Your job won't take care of you when you are sick. Your friends and parents will. Stay in touch. 5. Pay off your credit cards every month. 6. You don't have to win every argument. Agree to disagree. 7. Cry with someone. It's more healing than crying alone. 8. It's OK to get angry with God. He can take it. 9. Save for retirement starting with your first paycheck. 10. When it comes to chocolate, resistance is futile. 11. Make peace with your past so it won't screw up the present. 12. It's OK to let your children see you cry. 13. Don't compare your life to others. You have no idea what their journey is all about. 14. If a relationship has to be a secret, you shouldn't be in it. 15. Everything can change in the blink of an eye. But don't worry; God never blinks. 16. Take a deep breath. It calms the mind. 17. Get rid of anything that isn't useful, beautiful or joyful. 18. Whatever doesn't kill you really does make you stronger. 19. It's never too late to have a happy childhood. But the second one is up to you and no one else. 20. When it comes to going after what you love in life, don't take no for an answer. 21. Burn the candles, use the nice sheets, wear the fancy lingerie. Don't save it for a special occasion. Today is special. 22. Over prepare, then go with the flow. 23. Be eccentric now. Don't wait for old age to wear purple. 24. No one is in charge of your happiness but you. 25. Frame every so-called disaster with these words ''In five years, will this matter?''. 26. Always choose life. 27. Forgive everyone everything. 28. What other people think of you is none of your business. 29. Time heals almost everything. Give time, time. 30. However good or bad a situation is, it will change. 31. Don't take yourself so seriously. No one else does. 32. Believe in miracles. 33. God loves you because of who God is, not because of anything you did or didn't do. 34. Don't audit life. Show up and make the most of it now. 35. Growing old beats the alternative —dying young. 36. Your children get only one childhood. 37. All that truly matters in the end is that you loved. 38. Get outside every day. Miracles are waiting everywhere. 39. If we all threw our problems in a pile and saw everyone else's, we'd grab ours back. 40. Envy is a waste of time. You already have all you need. 41. The best is yet to come. 42. No matter how you feel, get up, dress up and show up. 43. Yield. 44. Life isn't tied with a bow, but it's still a gift. 45. Friends are the family that we choose for ourselves.

A BOOK LIST

I'm often asked what books I read. I like non-fiction, mysteries, novels, and I especially love memoirs. I like to read really good literature and books that critics say are examples of bad writing. I find it interesting to get a feel for how a subject is written. I'm in love with the written word and applaud anyone who takes the time and creates the discipline necessary to write. It takes courage to write—especially memoir. I agree with Stephen King's advice to writers: read a lot and write a lot. I also recommend collecting stories and quotes. I have journals filled with quotes that inspire me. Here is a short list of books I like:

    Brande, Dorothea: *Becoming a Writer*
    Crystal, Billy: *700 Sundays*
    Dahl, Roald: *Boy*
    Dillard, Annie: *An American Childhood*
    Estes, Clarissa: *Women Who Run with the Wolfs*
    Estess, Jenifer: *Talesr From the Bed*
    Ephron, Nora: *I Remember Nothing and Other Reflections*
    Faulkner, William: *As I Lay Dying*
    Goldberg, Natalie: *Old Friend From Far Away*
    Heilbrun, Carolyn: *Writing A Woman's Life*
    Hillman, James: *Dreams and the Underworld*
    Jung, Carl: *Memories, Dreams, Reflections*
    Kidd, Sue: *The Secret Life of Bees*
    King, Stephen: *On Writing*
    McCarthy, Mary: *Memories of a Catholic Girlhood*
    Maclean, Norman: *A River Runs Through It and Other Stories*
    McCourt, Frank: *Angela's Ashes*
    McDermott, Alice: *Charming Billy*
    Morgan, Richard: *Remembering Your Story*
    Nelson, Kenneth: *Thoughts of a Boy Growing Up*
    Ouwehand, Terre: *Writing Your Way to Wholeness*

Reichl, Ruth: *For You Mom, Finally*
Richards, M: *Childhood, Poetry, Pottery, and the Person*
Rico, Gabriele: *Writing the Natural Way*
Rohr, Richard: *Near Occasions of Grace*
Roseman, Janet: *The Way of the Woman Writer*
Quindlen, Anna: *Lots of Candles, Plenty of Cake*
Quindlen, Anna: *One True Thing*
Shapiro, Dani: *Devotion*
Stillman, Peter: *Families Writing*
Ueland, Brenda: *If You Want to Write*
Wakefield, Dan: *The Story of Your Life: Writing a Spiritual Autobiography*
Winner, Lauren: *Girl Meets God*
Winner, Lauren: *Still*

ABOUT THE AUTHOR

Sharon K. Ferrett, Emeritus Dean at Cal Poly Humboldt, has over forty-five years of experience in higher education as a college and university dean, director, professor and academic advisor. She is also a management consultant and a small business owner who brings this "real world" perspective to her presentations and books, Peak Performance, twelfth edition (McGraw-Hill, 2022), Positive Attitudes at Work (Irwin, 1994), Strategies: College and Career Success (Irwin 1996). Getting and Keeping the Job You Want, second edition (Irwin, 1995).

Sharon is a popular speaker on a variety of topics including; Working with Difficult People, Team Building, Motivation, Communication, Business Etiquette and Leadership, Creativity, Forgiveness, Peak Aging, Writing Memoir, Learning Styles and Skills, and Stress Management.

Sharon received her B.A. and M.A. in Communication from Western Michigan University, graduating Summa Cum Laude. She received her Ph.D. in higher education administration and organizational communication from Michigan State University. She also did graduate work at the University of Michigan, University of Edinburgh and University of London. Sharon and her husband Sam, former Mayor of Arcata, California, own an 1888 Victorian Bed and Breakfast in that town.

You can reach her at sharonferrett@gmail.com.

www.ingramcontent.com/pod-product-compliance
Lightning Source LLC
Chambersburg PA
CBHW060817050426
42449CB00008B/1702